ORIGINS OF TERRORISM

ORIGINS OF TERRORISM

The Rise of the World's Most Formidable Terrorist Groups

Godfrey Garner and Maeghin Alarid-Hughes

CRC Press
Taylor & Francis Group
Boca Raton London New York

CRC Press is an imprint of the
Taylor & Francis Group, an **informa** business

First edition published 2021
by CRC Press
6000 Broken Sound Parkway NW, Suite 300, Boca Raton, FL 33487-2742

and by CRC Press
2 Park Square, Milton Park, Abingdon, Oxon, OX14 4RN

© 2021 Taylor & Francis Group, LLC

CRC Press is an imprint of Taylor & Francis Group, LLC

ISBN: 978-0-367-47874-2 (hbk)
ISBN: 978-0-367-77186-7 (pbk)
ISBN: 978-1-003-17012-9 (ebk)

Typeset in Palatino
by MPS Limited, Dehradun

CONTENTS

PREFACE

Author's Note: Human nature is such that when contemplating another culture, one with which you are completely unfamiliar, the tendency is to assume a specific, shared behavior, that is, all white men such, all Native Americans such, etc. It's a common impulse and may only be overcome by conscious effort, and most people don't have the time or inclination to put forth such effort. Throughout this text, the authors will discuss some of these cultural behaviors in the context of academics and in an effort to encourage thought and conceptualized behavior on the part of the student. The information and data we (the authors) share with you are not speculative; however, and it must be understood that in addition to living among the population discussed and having conducted dozens of interviews over the years, collectively with members of the groups discussed in this text, we have additionally spent decades in the classroom and training scenarios imparting this knowledge to students and members of the military. In essence, we know what we're talking about. The material you read in this text is thoroughly researched and based on years of collective, personal experience. That said, it is up to the student to use common sense when studying this subject and realize that even the most widely accepted ideologies and practices among any culture cannot be applied to every member of that culture. We will not constantly point out throughout this text that the information we impart cannot be universally applied. This would be un-justifiably time-consuming. Just use basic common sense. We will restrict our material to that which we know from personal experience, that which we have researched and obtained from other experts in the field and that which we are confident enough about, to support with tried and established analysis.

Ask any ten Americans, with no connection to the world of counterterrorism, to provide a concise definition of terrorism, and you'll more than likely get ten completely different answers. This is not surprising when you consider that many professionals, many practitioners in the field of counterterrorism, still argue over the most accurate definition.

"Terrorism" is absolutely a relative term. Paradoxically, however, it is, in this day and age, easily recognized by most Americans.

The fact is that terrorism is a process used by individuals referred to naturally as terrorists who are not too unlike ourselves. Their actions are obviously reprehensible and foreign to us, but the emotions and the emotional responses to stimuli, stimuli that many of us also experience, are not that different from similar emotions and reactions we all have and feel.

They feel anger when they perceive they are wronged. They feel love for family and close friends. They feel loyalty and a sense of responsibility to be "loyal." In short, they aren't a great deal different from you or I, in this sense. This is by no means an attempt to make any sort of moral equivalence or offer anything resembling an excuse for their actions, but every intelligence analyst or operative will attest to the fact that defeating an enemy or controlling an adversary requires an understanding of that enemy/adversary and, to the greatest extent possible, an understanding of what drives them. This is much more easily accomplished when you make comparisons between the known (you and your own feelings and emotional responses to those feelings) and the unknown (those of the enemy/adversary).

Who precisely are "they"? There are hundreds of factors that go into a young person joining a terrorist group, and many of these factors are extremely innocuous. As such, they rarely come to mind as we, the uninitiated, have a tendency to complicate the "simple," especially when it is seemingly foreign to us. To begin with, there is the age-old eagerness of young men and women to join a cause, and unfortunately, this desire comes at a time when young people, mostly males (although a portion of this book will speak about females within terrorism as well), feel that emotional pull to "establish their identity."

When adults are asked the question, "who are you?" they will usually answer, in part, by stating what they do for a profession. Young people can't do this, but they observe it on a daily basis and equate it with the very basic definition of "adulthood." In this sense, becoming an adult, being a man or a woman, very subtly requires that you define yourself as to a calling or a profession or some other claim to fame. Young people begin this desperate search for "who they are," at about the same age young people in parts of the world are exposed to the "call to jihad." It's easy to see why some would make that leap into a "readymade" calling, a readymade token of manhood/womanhood.

That said, young people involved in terrorism can usually be separated into two major categories, those born to it and those who come late to it. By "born to it," we are referring to individuals who are exposed to and often indoctrinated into a type of Islamic fundamentalism from birth. For these individuals, that short step from religious zeal to violent extremism is just that, "short." Most among this first category are young men and women who are native Afghans, Arabs or Persians and who were born and raised in countries where the closest fundamentalist Imam preaches at a madrasa or mosque right around the corner.

They began learning their religion, as they should, at an early age, but for these individuals, the brand of Islam they begin learning is one laced liberally with a strong dose of what Christians might call "old time religion," a brand of religious zealotry that doesn't wince at the concept of "eradicating" those who do not subscribe to it. In fairness, though this type of fundamentalism does produce the majority of later practitioners of terrorism, it is not widely accepted among Muslims.[1]

The second category of terrorists is the "convert" to Islam, an experience that usually comes in early teen years. A fairly even mix of Protestants and Catholics, these young people are nonetheless, in large part, unfamiliar with Islam, and many have never even opened a Quran, let alone attempted to read or understand it. They are generally typical rebellious youth who yearn for adventure, a type of adventure they rarely understand. The zealotry that fuels them is often imagined, rather than foundationally supported by clearly understood religious principles, and magnified by the recruiters they happen to meet in person or online.

One cannot deny the simple fact, however, that a great deal of these young people are simply driven by the desire to dominate, often because they themselves have experienced domination by many they've grown up with and now see an opportunity to "turn the tables," this time supported and validated to some extent, though they don't understand how or why; young people seeking adventure or sex or both often become bullies, themselves grounded in the assumption that they are righteous in doing anything they want with and to the victims, the identified enemies of Islam.[2]

Additionally, those who see themselves as legitimate religious converts, such as the most well-known American jihadist, John Walker Lindh, as they are young and mostly ignorant of the actual religion of Islam, at this time in their lives, are most pliable and most prone to manipulation. It is often from this group that suicide actors are pulled.

One of the authors of this text, a veteran of both Vietnam and Afghanistan, once interviewed a convicted jihadist. The young man, knowing the author was a veteran of both wars, went to great lengths to justify his own actions, comparing them to the actions of the author when he was a younger man. The comparison, though twisted and manipulated, was easily misunderstood as valid, based on the perception of the young, former terrorist.

Most often, however, the real, perceived zeal and religious commitment, which hasn't been inculcated from birth, has a way of diminishing or disappearing altogether once the pain of combat is realized. As such, the recruiter and managers of the groups these individuals align themselves with usually attempt to get the most out of them early in their "terror career." The individuals we will study in this text however will be the individuals from category one. This category has produced the terror cell leaders and the most committed terrorists.

While the most common portion of the population to be radicalized and recruited by terrorist groups is young men, we will provide vital anecdotal data and analysis of the women who are drawn to these groups as well. We will also structure this material from the authors' experiences and material obtained from open source analysis, in order to allow the student to gain valuable insight into the relationships between many of the most widely known leaders of terrorist organizations.

In this text, we will examine some of these aforementioned emotions and the all-too-often common stimuli that trigger them. We will also, as stated, analyze the interrelationships among various terror leaders throughout the world: how their paths have crossed, how they have influenced one another and how this has (in part) shaped the individual terror leaders and the terror threats we see today.

It is important to realize that terrorist leaders have always been successful in organizing effective and long-lasting terror groups because they first experienced stimuli that led primarily to the emotional responses of anger and a sense of loss of control. They have also been able to recognize those same emotional responses in others, fuel them to their benefit and manage them by exercising above-average leadership skills. It is worth noting at this point that the terrorist leaders, such as bin Laden and Mullah Omar of the world of terrorism, are not that much different in this sense than Gandhi or Martin Luther King, Jr. in terms of these specific abilities and skills.[3] You, the reader, are now aghast by the previous sentence. You are now re-reading that sentence because you can't believe what you just read – a comparison between a terrorist and Gandhi? The authors want to stress emphatically that the only comparison that is being made is that Osama bin Laden, Mullah Omar and many other terror leaders were driven initially by the same emotions that fueled Gandhi and King (minimization, belittlement and degradation, which engendered anger and frustration). These men further capitalized on the same emotions in their followers and used highly similar leadership skills to accomplish their goals. They differed only but vastly in their goals and objectives and their methods of achieving those goals and objectives.

> *Author's Note: In addition to identifying the progression and certain milestones in the development and growth of actual terrorist groups and organizations, we will also cover simultaneous political events, mostly American in nature, since America has been among the most prevalent western targets of Islamic terror organizations. It is important to detail and expand upon what was happening behind the scenes in terrorist organizations, but it is also important to do much the same with our processes and how we undertook and have continued to undertake the fight against Islamic extremism. Unfolding events throughout history have been equally dependent on both the terrorists and the (American) adversary of the terrorist. When examining how and why we did the things we did and are doing, it is important to take a look at seemingly unrelated political events, that is, President Bill Clinton was highly influenced in how he allowed the search for Osama bin Laden to proceed, by political difficulties he was experiencing vis-a-vis "the Monica Lewinsky Affair." President George Bush the second was equally influenced by seemingly unrelated events that unfolded during his father's administration. This is not an attempt to criticize, but it is an attempt to understand the "whys and the hows" in both camps.*

NOTES

1 Islamic fundamentalism. (n.d.). In *Wikipedia*. https://en.wikipedia.org/wiki/Islamic_fundamentalism.

2 John Walker Lindh. (n.d.). In *Wikipedia*. https://en.wikipedia.org/wiki/John_Walker_Lindh.

3 Shaffer, R. (2018). Changes and drivers in contemporary terrorism. *Terrorism and Political Violence, 30*(3), 544–552. https://www.tandfonline.com/doi/full/10.1080/09546553.2018.1440047.

AUTHORS

Dr. Godfrey Garner is a professor at Mississippi College and adjunct professor at Tulane University, and Belhaven University teaching Counterterrorism and Intelligence Analysis for the Homeland Security degree programs. Dr. Garner is Director for Mississippi College Center for Counterterror Studies and is a locally recognized authority on terrorism, counter-terrorism and conflicts in the Middle East. His work, more than 150 professional articles and commentaries, has appeared in various newspapers and periodicals including *Homeland Security Today, American Diplomacy,* and *Foreign Policy Journal.* He is the author of the novels *The Balance of Exodus, Danny Kane and the Hunt for Mullah Omar, Clothed in White Raiment, Brothers in the Mekong Delta* and coauthor of the textbook, *Intelligence Analysis Fundamentals,* published by Taylor & Francis Group/CRC Press. He served in Vietnam and Afghanistan and completed two military and eight civilian government, intelligence and counterintelligence related tours in Afghanistan.

Maeghin Alarid-Hughes earned an MA in International Security and Homeland Defense and a graduate certificate in Terrorism Analysis. She is an Adjunct Professor in Terrorism and Risk Analysis for Arapahoe Community College out of Colorado. She is a subject matter expert and consultant in Counter-terrorism for Guidepoint. She was the Project Coordinator for Project Arrowhead, a Department of Homeland Security-funded countering violent extremism project through Mississippi College. She was the lead policy analyst at the Institute for National Security Studies onsite at the Air Force Academy in Colorado Springs, working for arms control, nonproliferation and strategic stability issues for the Air Force. She has 15 years of experience working for the Department of Defense, the Defense Threat Reduction Agency and every branch of the military. She was a terrorism instructor at the Defense Nuclear Weapons School where she created the school's first course on Female Suicide Bombers. She was asked to present her research on Female Recruitment and Radicalization Online at the Women's Peace and Security Conference in 2015. Her research was published in the book *Impunity: Countering Illicit Power in War and Transition* by the National Defense University. She is also a contributing author in the book *Online Terrorist Propaganda, Recruitment, and Radicalization* by CRC Press. She has worked in countering violent extremism and social media monitoring for the last nine years. She has worked with State, Federal and Military first responders as well as international students and has traveled to various military bases throughout the United States instructing response to radiological terrorism.

1

Insurgency, Religion and Terrorist Relationships

INSURGENCY AND ITS RELATIONSHIP TO TERRORISM

Throughout this text, we will refer to the concept of "insurgency." The concept and evolution of insurgency movements are so important to this text and narrative because "terrorism" is used most often to accomplish the objectives of the insurgent, and most terrorists would refer to themselves as "insurgents," a term that, relatively speaking, carries with it a nobler connotation.

"Insurgency": this simple word has led to some of the longest-lasting wars and the heaviest tolls in loss of life in the history of mankind. Some experts would assert that insurgency movements have killed more people than the most prolific plagues known to man.

In its simplest form, an insurgency is a movement that develops when a group of people are dissatisfied with the leadership of their country and want to depose it, that is, when a change is sought. Actions of terrorist groups are all directed toward effecting a change of some type, and an insurgency is a process that seeks the greatest change.

Insurgencies generally begin benignly at the ballot box if such exists in the particular country. If unsuccessful, it evolves into force, as frustration grows. As the movement expands, the local government assisted by any allies conducts "counterinsurgency" operations to defeat the movement. The most important aspect of any insurgency/counterinsurgency is the people. The more the people (citizens of the country)

1

side with the insurgent movement, the more is the likelihood of success. Adversely, the more the people resist, or side with the government, the more likely the movement will fail. Without the support of the people, an insurgency cannot survive.

We often refer to an insurgency/counterinsurgency as two beaus trying to woo the same girl. The beaus being the "two movements (insurgents and counterinsurgents), and the girl metaphorically being the people." As is often the case, the beaus use "carrots" to woo the girl, "come with us, we provide a better life for you." If however this doesn't work, the beaus may switch to the "stick" (research will show that most often the "insurgents" signify the beaus who are most willing to shift to the "stick"): "you'll come with us, or else."

As said, governments do this (use the stick) as well, but they aren't as likely or as quick to resort to such, because they wield more power than the insurgents. Finally, "putting a bow on it," insurgent groups that last long without achieving the stated goals, especially in Islamic countries, at some point become terrorist groups, resorting to terrorism to achieve their objectives. With Islamic extremist terror groups such as Al Qaeda and Islamic State (Daesh), the objective (the change sought) is to attain a pure Islamic state, "pure" the way they perceive it. Terrorism is used to achieve this objective because no other means, as far as they're concerned, exist for them.

An insurgency is a movement that has its beginning in simple frustration. A good, recent example is the "Arab Spring" movement, which, though highly successful in the beginning, met a wall in Syria, which led to the Syrian civil war which to date has taken the lives of a half million men, women and children and shows no sign of abating. There was little appetite among the young people who launched the movement initially to become terrorists, and of course, as they met with much success early on, there was no need for it. However, the fact is that the government of Syria has been extremely ruthless and barbaric in handling the movement. For his part, Bashar al-Assad, the Syrian President, would argue that the rebels, or insurgents, are nothing more than terrorists.

The Arab Spring movement began in spring 2011 (spark was lit in December 2010) in Tunisia when an elderly street vendor, who used to sell vegetables on the street for years, set himself on fire because the government seized his vendor cart and forced him off the street. The ensuing demonstrations caused the Tunisian leader to abdicate and flee the country, and all this happened in a very short period of time. The movement quickly spread to Egypt and Libya, meeting with similar success. When it developed in Syria, however, a full-scale civil war erupted that continues till today.[1]

Another example of a successful insurgency is that which took place in Vietnam. This insurgency took the lives of millions before it ended in unification of north and south, in 1975; again, a successful insurgency that was birthed in a moment of frustration.

In short, an insurgency is a rebellion against existing rule. It is carried out by individuals referred to as insurgents. Some would say an insurgent can also be referred to as a "freedom fighter," but the choice of either term is strictly a relative one. It is entirely in the mind of the beholder, which brings up the principal problem in conducting a successful insurgency, gaining support and agreement from those most affected. Every insurgency faces the problem of convincing those affected (the citizens) to join the process. Successful insurgencies are successful because the majority of the people support them, by choice or because they are forced or coerced into support.

The consideration of "freedom fighters vs. terrorists" is very convoluted. Even Ronald Reagan spoke of this in a 1985 speech. The topic is the subject of countless journal articles and research papers and has been debated back and forth among those in the defense arena. Some scholars argue that freedom fighters or terrorism is "justifiable" provided it adheres to the "Just War" criteria.

Michael Walzer, a historian who wrote *Just and Unjust Wars* (1977), describes this as terrorism being permissible under "extreme emergencies."[2] The most interesting point in this work, "one person's freedom fighter is someone else's terrorist," is that the perceptions of individuals involved are often based on their geographic proximity to the actions of the freedom fighters/terrorists. If this is happening in your own backyard, or you are the target of the action, you may look at a group as terrorists. If you are on the other side of the world and removed from the direct actions of the group, you may see them as freedom fighters. As an example, Israelis may see the Palestinian Liberation Organization as terrorists, but those far-removed from the conflict may feel Palestinians have a right to a homeland and call the group freedom fighters.

An insurgency begins as stated, through frustration against the current leadership of a country. This frustration grows until it evolves into resistance. This resistance may materialize as peaceful or violent (most insurgencies begin as peaceful movements). Mahatma Gandhi and Martin Luther King, for instance, led peaceful and successful insurgencies. As stated, the aforementioned Arab Spring insurgency began as peaceful resistance, but led to civil war.

Al Qaeda, though it began in Pakistan as a support movement for the mujahideen fighting against the Russians in Afghanistan, quickly became a terror organization, following withdrawal of Russian troops from that country. Most analysts believe that Osama bin Laden intended the development of Al Qaeda all along, but the focus had nothing to do with the war in Afghanistan. His intent all along was resistance to the Saudi Royal Family's embracing of the west, and the opportunity presented itself when Saddam Hussain invaded Kuwait. As it developed, bin Laden very simply made the calculated decision to use acts of terror to accomplish his goals (Figure 1.1).

His hatred was directed primarily toward the United States and its allies, but it began as a hatred for and a resistance against his own country. We will see, as we go forward, this same pattern evolving with most of the other organized terror groups: resistance, insurgency and terrorism.

Figure 1.1 Arab Spring protests in Taiz, Yemen, February 2011. (Source: www.shutterstock.com; Used with permission).

RELIGION AND ITS ROLE IN ISLAMIC EXTREMISM

From the beginning of this text, we have been and will continue to provide examples in order to allow the student of this most important subject to better understand the context. This section will delve into the impact certain interpretations of Islam have, and will continue to have, on extremism. It is an understatement to point out that the worst of any religion lies in its interpretation, and Islam is certainly not insulated from this. As a matter of fact, various interpretations of the Prophet Mohammad's intent on basically all matters and questions (e.g., what did he intend in taking this action or declaring this) are possibly more varied and confusing than those of any other religion, Christianity included. Every religion has, to varying degrees, extremist-driven narratives that more often than not cause hardship. Think of "what you know and understand" when you are reading about and studying "what you don't know, or understand."

Islam in America, the UK, or even Saudi Arabia is so vastly different from Islam in Afghanistan as it seems to be a different religion altogether. This section however will focus on what the authors know about Islam in Afghanistan since that region provides a framework for most of the extremist groups in the world today.

Initially, the reader must understand that Islam and its guiding principles, as well as the perceived (word "perceived" is vitally important) intent of the Prophet Mohammad and the Quran and Hadith, are all encompassing in Afghanistan. Islam controls every facet of life, especially in the back country. Nothing, absolutely nothing, is done without first considering the Quran or the Hadith or simply what is universally understood about Islam and its principles.

Business is not conducted without it, governmental functions are not performed without it, and simple daily interactions with a neighbor or a family member for that matter are not conducted without it. To ask that Islam takes a back seat to any other consideration is asking a fish to forgo the use of water.

This is both a good thing and a bad thing. The importance of religious advisors present at all times to "advise" terrorist leaders as to their actions has been a guiding factor in everything from negotiations to suicide attacks and plays that same role today. Terror leaders such as the late Osama bin Laden, Mullah Mohammad Omar and Musab Zarqawi all kept their "favorite, preferred" mullah or spiritual advisor close at hand throughout all their operations. Zarqawi, for instance, consulted a spiritual advisor before he ordered the suicide attack on a Jordanian wedding celebration that killed hundreds of men, women, and children. He no doubt slept well afterward knowing he was within the will of Allah.

The bad thing about such dogmatic adherence to a religious philosophy is that it removes the need for moral consideration or self-restraint or guidance of the individual conscience. If your spiritual advisor tells you that it is Allah's will that you kidnap and rape Yazidi girls as young as 14 but no younger, then there's no reason to think the matter through. This was a common practice by ISIS. They kidnapped numerous Yazidi women and young girls and forced them into sexual slavery; according to them, it is all within the bounds of Islam.

Another compelling factor along these lines specific to the country of Afghanistan, particularly in the regions away from the cities, is extreme poverty. People who haven't experienced it the way Afghans in the villages experience it lose sight of the physical toll it takes on one, just to survive and to feed families. This is vitally important because moral considerations, matters of the conscience and right vs. wrong are all matters that require energy and effort to consider. It's much easier just to follow the guidance than to take the time and effort to conceptualize or mentally debate. The local Mullah will tell you what's right. Just do it and don't waste time and energy thinking about it.

Off the subject slightly, but this is a prime reason "democracy" has never worked well and probably never will work well in the "back country." Most people don't realize it, but "democracy" on the part of individuals involves mental and often physical efforts, and there's very little of that available, especially when the rewards are never considered to be worth the effort.

Another benefit of this adherence to strict interpretations of Islam, however, is that many young people can be swayed at times by a cogent argument using the Quran. One of the authors of this text has been involved in interrogations in which young people have changed their focus because of logical arguments and explanations as to the error of their Islamic interpretations or the error of their ways. The Jordanian Mukabarat (counterterror unit) was often successful in the early days, in influencing Musab Zarqawi, before he became the rock star persona in the terror world that would supersede all else until his death.

Finally, on this subject, Afghans, especially rural Afghans who of course make up the vast majority of the country's people, are completely convinced that their brand of Islam is the only pure Islam and that all other Muslims are inferior in their spirituality and their daily life. This has caused and will cause strife with other nations. Even when Saudi fighters went to Afghanistan to assist the mujahideen against the Russians, such turmoil and infighting over religious matters often hindered their efforts.

TERRORISTS AS ALLIES/RELATIONSHIPS BETWEEN TERRORISTS AND TERRORIST ORGANIZATIONS

When terror groups band together, it is in the best interest of both groups. We have seen such alliances occur between groups such as the Popular Front for the Liberation of Palestine (PFLP) and the Japanese Red Army (JRA) for example.

Asal et al. (2015) state about this in their research titled, "With Friends like These … Why Terrorist Organizations Ally." The uniting force between the PFLP and the JRA rested upon a foundation of their communist worldviews. As Asal et al. state:

> *"Alliances tend to form between organizations that share motivation (especially if the potential partners are both Islamic or both ethno-nationalist in their motivation), are relatively similar in age, seek to target the same country, are drawn from the same region, and are based in countries with small militaries. Overall, terrorist organizations tend to prefer network structures that are organized into cliques or subgroups, though with some outreach to clusters beyond their primary partners."[3]*

Asal et al. raise important questions about alliances between terror groups and what is imperative about those alliances. They ask if ideological connections are the most important factor when considering aligning forces, does regional proximity take precedence, or is the exchange of resources, skills, knowledge and expertise more crucial?

> *"(1) terrorists exchange among themselves technologies and techniques that are unique to terrorism and (2) there are behavioral implications of terrorists relating to one another—for instance, well-connected organizations are more likely to kill, more likely to kill prolifically, and more likely to pursue weapons of mass destruction."[3] Even Osama bin Laden aligned himself*

with other groups such as the Taliban and made a deal with
them prior to 9/11 that would benefit both the Taliban and Al
Qaeda. The Taliban provided refuge for bin Laden inside
Afghanistan, but (as many analysts believe) made it clear to him
that he could not "use Afghanistan to conduct a freelance war
against America."[4]

In his book, *Man Hunt*, Peter Bergen spoke about the relationship between Al Qaeda and the Taliban as follows: "As plans for the 9/11 attacks took a more definite shape, some of Al Qaeda's senior officials expressed concern that the coming attacks might anger the Taliban leader Mullah Omar, to whom bin Laden had, at least notionally, sworn an oath of allegiance. During the five years that bin Laden had been the Taliban's honored guest, Mullah Omar and other Taliban leaders had made it clear that Al Qaeda could not use Afghanistan to conduct a freelance war against America."[4]

The Taliban wanted the Northern Alliance leader, Ahmad Shah Masood (an infamous anti-Taliban resistance leader), dead for quite some time. Bin Laden promised to assassinate Masood if the Taliban looked the other way after the 9/11 attacks. Masood was assassinated in a suicide bombing attack, by two Arab fighters brought in from Saudi Arabia, at the direction of Osama bin Laden. Posing as TV journalists seeking an interview with the famous Northern Alliance leader, two days before the attacks of 9/11, they asked, during the interview, the first question and then activated a trigger device, detonating explosives hidden in the camera.

It's fascinating to examine relationships between various terrorist groups as well as those within the same terror organization. We have all heard the name Ayman al-Zawahiri since he took over as leader of Al Qaeda after the death of bin Laden. Zawahiri had been embedded with bin Laden and Al Qaeda since its inception. He was not a household name initially because of his preference to remain behind the scenes. Even today, he is a quiet man who doesn't seem keen to remain in the limelight.

He is highly intelligent, an Egyptian physician and has over the years often been referred to as the "brain" behind bin Laden. Despite his high rank and the respect and trust that bin Laden bestowed upon him, Zawahiri was not privy to the knowledge and planning of the 9/11 attacks until a few months prior to them occurring.[5]

Zawahiri is not the charismatic leader as bin Laden was. In numerous books about bin Laden, it has been pointed out that he (bin Laden) was an extremely charismatic leader. He was eloquent and charming.

The fact that he gave up a life of luxury to lead Al Qaeda and spent his days on the run only made him more endearing to his followers.

Al Qaeda was at its peak when bin Laden was the leader. The terrorist group has declined since his demise for many reasons (including many fighters killed by US and ally forces, a decrease in funding and morale, etc.). Another reason for the reduction in size and effectiveness of Al Qaeda is that Zawahiri has never been considered a compelling leader, capable of bringing fresh young recruits to the organization. Unlike bin Laden, Zawahiri failed to attract the young recruits who instead flocked to ISIS to pledge their allegiance. Another potential factor is age. Zawahiri is older than Zarqawi (the first ISIS leader) and Zarqawi's successors. Zawahiri and his "old school" ways have not been seen as sexy, exciting and promising life of adventure, all essential requirements that an organization like ISIS needs to lure new recruits.

ISIS promised all these things to their recruits and hence has seen thousands upon thousands of young people drawn to their message and supportive of their methods of operation. At one time, Al Qaeda members and leaders had placed their hope on the future of the organization in the leadership ability of Hamza bin Laden, son of Osama. This hope vanished when Hamza was killed sometime between 2017 and 2019 (Figure 1.2).[6]

Figure 1.2 Hamza bin Laden, Osama bin Laden's son.

To date, although Al Qaeda is still active and may once again prove to be a dominant terrorist organization, it will need a complete overhaul of their branding, message and methods. ISIS and Al Qaeda both have shared a goal (to rid their land of the west and establish Sharia law), but their methods were irreconcilable, a fact that has led to a volatile relationship between the two groups.

While bin Laden inspired his followers from the depths of dank and dingy caves with little to no earthly possessions (save weapons and ammunition), ISIS and their former leader Abu Bakr al-Baghdadi promised their recruits a life of adventure and action on the front lines. While Al Qaeda taught piety and patience, ISIS proclaimed "a woman for every fighter," weapons training and a place on the front lines of the action with a view to take "revenge against the West." Thus, ISIS saw an influx of young people flock to their group. Essentially, their message made it sound like in joining ISIS, recruits would "have their cake and eat it too." They would not have to give up their modern conveniences, would gain a life of purpose and power and would tackle the West with the tit-for-tat strategy, while gaining the favor of Allah and securing a place for themselves in Heaven. Al Qaeda promised a chance to fulfill the will of Allah, but little more.

Al Qaeda recruits were generally older; however, many were seasoned fighters and "old school" jihadis who had often been imprisoned for a time that intensified their level of radicalization. Additionally, Al Qaeda recruits preferred the simple message of Al Qaeda and did not shy away from a life of frugality and travel between remote areas. All this has worked out well for Al Qaeda in the past, but if a terrorist organization is to survive past one generation, one must have a message that resonates with the young (Figure 1.3).

Author's Note: "Al Qaeda in Iraq's (the predecessor of ISIS; ISIS in its infancy, led by a young Musab Zarqawi) indiscriminate violence often targeting fellow Sunnis, eventually led to a backlash from the Sunni tribes that, when combined with the 2006 U.S. troop "surge" in Iraq, hit the group hard. For Al Qaeda, this was a broader disaster, with the Iraqi group's setbacks and abuses tarnishing the overall jihadist cause. Indeed, in private, Al Qaeda spokesman Adam Gadahn recommended to bin Laden that Al Qaeda publicly "sever its ties" with Al Qaeda in Iraq because of the group's sectarian violence."[7]

Figure 1.3   Abu Musab Zarqawi.

Two terror groups competing for dominance in one area will never peacefully coexist, just as rival drug gangs do not simply "let the other be."

NOTES

1 History. (2018, January 10). *Arab Spring*. Retrieved May 12, 2020, from https:// www.history.com/topics/middle-east/arab-spring.
2 Walzer, M. (2015). *Just and unjust wars: A moral argument with historical illustrations*. Basic Books.
3 Asal, V. H., Park, H. H., Rethemeyer, R. K., & Ackerman, G. (2015). With friends like these … why terrorist organizations ally. *International Public Management Journal, 19*(1), 1–30.
4 Bergen, P. (2012). *Manhunt: The ten-year search for Bin Laden from 9/11 to Abbottabad*, (p. 19). Crown Publishers.
5 Bergen, P. (2012). *Manhunt: The ten-year search for Bin Laden from 9/11 to Abbottabad*, (p. 22). Crown Publishers.
6 Gonzales, R. (2019, July 31). Hamza Bin Laden, son of Osama Bin Laden, is reported dead. *NPR*. https://www.npr.org/2019/07/31/747050559/hamza-bin-laden-son-of-osama-bin-laden-is-reported-dead.
7 https://www.brookings.edu/testimonies/comparing-AlQaeda-and-isis-different-goals-different-targets/.

2

Terror Mind Manipulation

WHY TERROR; WHY TERROR GROUPS: A MANIPULATION OF THE MIND

Terrorism and acts of terror are used to accomplish one of two types of objectives, political or religious. Occasionally, the lines between these two are crossed, but most often the objective is one or the other. Political acts of terror, for instance, were seen in America during the civil rights era and the protests against the war in Vietnam.

In terms of counterterrorism, it is much easier to control or defeat a politically motivated terrorist or terror campaign than it is to defeat a religiously motivated one, for obvious reasons. Those motivated by religious objectives have less fear of dying and, in some cases, actively seek *shahadat* as the act of martyrdom. Politically motivated terrorists such as Ilich Ramirez Sanchez (Carlos the Jackal; he was politically and materially motivated since he often hired out) rarely seek death and are, therefore, by comparison slightly less dangerous.

Terrorism is useful in that it can be highly effective in negating the effects of the most powerful weapon human beings have: the "human mind." Members of the military, especially those who've gone through the most rigorous training for special operations units such as the US Navy SEALs and Army Special Forces, know that the one thing that can get them through the training successfully is their strength of mind and the emotional resolve it provides. Actually, the mind is the one thing that has allowed human beings, in a multitude of scenarios historically, to survive and emerge victorious when faced with overwhelming odds. The mind can give us victory. It can also defeat us.

Acts of terror are designed to cause chaos and confusion, and in doing so, they defeat the resolve of the mind and negate the victory available through a positive, strong will. In the aforementioned special operations training, chaos and confusion are often introduced into training situations to teach trainees to adapt.

The devastatingly effective combination of chaos and confusion undermines us. It robs us of confidence and instills fear. It works. Terror organizations usually attempt to induce chaos and confusion in a situation, since it is in this environment that they stand the greatest chance of success, but they also look for opportunities where such chaos and confusion are naturally present, such as in the case of the civil war in Syria. The human mind cannot steal itself against an adversarial situation if it can't grasp or understand it to some degree. Chaotic situations slow the resolve of the mind, and when chaos is amplified through the use of mass violence, the strength and resolve of the mind deteriorate further. Again, it works.

Terrorist groups rise up continuously all over the world because their various followers truly believe in their cause, their creed and their tactics.

"Terrorist leaders believe that terrorism truly is effective in defeating the occupying or foreign dominant peoples."[1]

We often see terrorists as mentally ill and moronic individuals with extensive criminal records. The reality is that those that join or start terror groups, much like leaders of a cult, have a skewed vision for utopia and are highly misinformed about those they perceive as "others." They may or may not have previously engaged in criminal activity. They most certainly perceive that they, themselves or their people, have been "wronged" and are victims of great injustices. As a matter of fact, recruitment of individuals to terror organizations (Islamic-based terror organizations) follow a form of indoctrination that generally patterns itself with the assurance that the prospective recruit (1) is a member of an extended family that includes all the nations of the world, (2) has brothers in each of these countries, who (3) are being oppressed and often murdered by those who oppose pure Islam and finally (4) need their help.

Insofar as terror, historically its use in war has been frowned upon. It has, however, been used to various extents by most nations. The practice is often referred to as Psychological Operations (PSYOPS). During WWII for instance, British-trained Nepalese Ghurka soldiers used tactics that were designed specifically to induce terror in the enemy. Ghurka soldiers were used under contract to the East India Company in the Pindaree War of 1817, in Bharatpur in 1826 and in the First and Second Anglo-Sikh Wars in 1846 and 1848.[2] During the Indian Rebellion of 1857, Gurkhas fought on the British Side and became part of the British Indian Army on its formation.

With a cry of *"Ayo Gorkhali!"* (The Gurkhas are upon you), British Ghurka soldiers during WWII would instill terror in their adversaries. They were known for sneaking into the foxholes of their enemies in the dead quiet of night and slitting the throat of one of the occupants, escaping unnoticed and unheard. The terror induced by such a sight as others awoke to the following day succinctly answers the question, "why terror?"

Even America, during the Vietnam conflict, used "ghost patrols" to instill terror in the hearts of Vietcong and NVA soldiers conducting operations in the jungles of South Vietnam in the dead and dark of night. One of the authors of this text was operationally involved in many of these very operations.

As the Vietnamese culture lends itself to a strong belief in the existence of spirits, both gentle and malevolent, American patrols would enter the jungles by way of the canals, at night, in areas where VC and NVA operations were thought to be active, and play ghost stories complete with eerie music, on loudspeakers, detailing how certain spirits were roaming the jungles that very night in search of a replacement head, for the one they lost when they were killed. It sounds puerile to an extent, but the fact is that such patrols always resulted in at least one or two *chu hois* (surrenders) and, normally, at least one pretty good firefight.[3]

While there is a vast difference between WWII British Ghurka, American and Vietnam operations and the acts of terror carried out on 9/11 by Al Qaeda operatives, over and above the fact that the 9/11 victims were non-combatants, as are the typical victims of present-day acts of terror, the basic effects and reasoning behind the use of terror are the same; it works.

We all have a multitude of questions as to why and how acts of terror occur and are seemingly increasing in number around the world. This text will answer some of those questions but will do so by delving into the lives of some of the organizers of the most prolific terror groups and illustrating the thought process and reasoning that is specific to some of them and typical of most of them.

Author's Note: It is recommended by the authors of this text that the students use a timeline (personalized to individual students)

15

*in order to more easily keep major historic terrorism-related acts
in proper temporal relation. For instance, knowing what was
happening in Afghanistan, when Ahmad al-Khalayleh (Zarqawi)
was becoming radicalized in Jordan, provides a whole new
perspective and level of interest. A linear timeline of the reader's
preference is recommended. This will allow a quick reference and
may even provide some insight into motivations of certain individuals. An example timeline is shown in Figure 2.1, though
since this is individualized, the student should design one that
works for them. The overall purpose is generating a process
whereby the student has a mental picture of the period of time
when notable events happened. This is much easier when the
student can compare the "unknown" with the "known," for instance, "when I began high school, Osama bin Laden was just
arriving in Pakistan to assist with the Afghan war with
Russia," or "the year I graduated from high school, Musab
Zarqawi was beginning to organize Al Qaeda in Iraq." The
timeline should be personalized for each student in order to
make it easiest to establish, update and navigate.*

This topic was discussed earlier, but it is vitality important that the
students of International Terrorism and its history understand the concept of insurgency and counterinsurgency in light of the fact that successful "insurgency operations" leading to a successful "insurgent"
campaign are more often than not the ultimate objective of terror groups.

Again, as discussed in previous chapters, an "insurgency" and its
opposite (counterinsurgency) are occasionally described as two beaus
vying for the affection of the same girl. It is also described as a "winning
of the hearts and mind" type action, since the objective is to convince the
populace to choose the insurgents over the counterinsurgents as the
ruling entity of the country.

Vietnam was a classic insurgency/counterinsurgency action. If
through insurgency operations, a group can win over the larger, non-
combatant populace, that populace will reject the opposing side and the
objectives of the insurgent will have been accomplished. Insurgents use
the "carrot and the stick" in such operations. Obviously, the "stick" is
"terror operations."

Today, in Afghanistan, the Taliban is still operational (Taliban is a
"regional" as opposed to "international" terror organization. This will be
discussed in more detail later in Chapter 7), providing "shadow

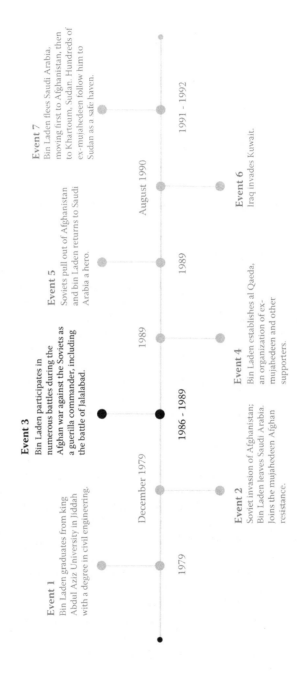

Event 1
Bin Laden graduates from king Abdul Aziz University in Jiddah with a degree in civil engineering.

1979

Event 2
Soviet invasion of Afghanistan; Bin Laden leaves Saudi Arabia. Joins the mujahedeen Afghan resistance.

December 1979

Event 3
Bin Laden participates in numerous battles during the Afghan war against the Soviets as a guerilla commander, including the battle of Jalalabad.

1986 - 1989

Event 4
Bin Laden establishes al Qaeda, an organization of ex-mujahedeen and other supporters.

1989

Event 5
Soviets pull out of Afghanistan and bin Laden returns to Saudi Arabia a hero.

1989

August 1990

Event 6
Iraq invades Kuwait.

Event 7
Bin Laden flees Saudi Arabia, moving first to Afghanistan, then to Khartoum, Sudan. Hundreds of ex-mujahedeen follow him to Sudan as a safe haven.

1991 - 1992

Figure 2.1 A sample timeline useful in visualizing relevant events.

17

government" functions to the more extreme locales of the country, while conducting suicide attack operations in order to generate chaos in those areas that refute their authority. Understanding insurgency operations will provide the reader of this text a more grounded concept of "why" the use of terror, and help in getting to know a bit more regarding the mind of the terrorist and the terror leader.

THAT'S NOT FAIR

This section is devoted to that old question we've asked ourselves since adolescence, namely, "what the heck was I thinking?" Most westerners, when broaching the question of terrorism, focus their thoughts and interrogatories in the direction of "why would someone do this." The question becomes more important and relevant considering the fact that large numbers of terrorists join terrorist organizations even after knowing that it will lead to their death or imprisonment.

Understanding this is much easier when you delineate subgroups of terrorists and would-be terrorists. The first category of subgroup separation is those who grew up in a strict Islamic environment, that is Saudi Arabia, Afghanistan or any other Middle Eastern, predominantly Islamic, countries, as opposed to those who did not, and therefore came to Islam and were religiously converted, later in life.

Young men and women who grow up in Afghanistan, Syria or Saudi, for instance, are naturally exposed to an environment that focuses on religion: Islam, first and foremost, and all other matters second. Simple daily questions, considerations and decisions examine religious implications first followed by all other issues. Islam is of course the government as well as the principal religion. For these young people, *shahadat* (religious martyrdom) is not such a strange concept. Joining and fighting for an Islamist organization such as Al Qaeda, Taliban or ISIS is not so strange. Struggling for the reestablishment of the Caliphate and worldwide dominance by Islam, or strict adherence to Sharia is more of a foregone conclusion.

When you couple this with the fact that many of these Middle Eastern countries, especially Afghanistan, are very poor and the young people in these areas grow up with few options, it is easier to understand how a young person could devote him or herself to such activities. One of the authors had an opportunity to talk to some would-be suicide bombers in Afghanistan and Iraq, and one thing prevalent among them was the sheer sadness and heartbreaking disappointment they expressed when they knew they had to continue living and had been denied the rewards of *shahadat*. Their experiences leading up to affiliation with terror organizations were much different from the kid in New York City who converted to Islam from a predominantly Catholic family and eventually joined a group loosely affiliated with ISIS.

Another issue that is of importance and that escapes the knowledge and understanding of the NYC kid is the relationship and the vast gulf between Sunni Muslims and Shiite Muslims. Such a difference has historically fueled many of the most vicious acts of terrorism. Ahmad al-Khalayleh (Musab al-Zarqawi, organizer of Al Qaeda in Iraq which led to formation of ISIS) orchestrated the killing of thousands and thousands of Muslims in the process of organizing ISIS and attempting to thwart the efforts of American forces in Northern Iraq, simply because they were Shiite Muslims. He was also attempting to draw US forces into untenable situations, but the hatred of Shiite Muslims made it a little easier for him and his followers.

The issue here is that the kid from NYC probably couldn't explain the difference between the two. In short, their trip to radicalization was a much different one, and this needs to be understood if you're going to try to figure out "what were they thinking."

Most people can tell you who John Walker Lindh was, but few are aware of his circuitous route from a high school kid in San Francisco to America's own Taliban. Lindh grew up in San Francisco as a member of a fairly affluent family. He excelled in school learning Arabic with remarkably little difficulty.

John Lindh grew up in a Catholic family and was exposed to a hefty dose of chaos and turmoil in his family during adolescence. His father often left the family to go live with a male lover, eventually divorcing his mother and moving in with the lover in 1999. The year before however, at 16, Lindh left the family and traveled to Yemen, having converted to Islam. There is no indication that he went there to join an Islamist group, and as a matter of fact, it is highly likely that he knew little of the Taliban, the group he eventually fought with and was captured with.

Following a period of time studying in Yemen, he returned home but soon left again and traveled to Pakistan for more studying. From interrogation data, we know that he still hadn't planned to join any organized group such as the Taliban. He was however upset because his fellow students in Pakistan didn't take their studies as seriously as he did. As a result, he left Pakistan to travel across the border and join the Taliban, but

19

some indications are that he did so primarily because they were a pious Islamic organization. Soon, however, he found himself with a gun in his hand and had no problem taking up arms against his fellow Americans.

Michael Spann, a CIA agent, was the first American to be killed in Afghanistan in OEF (Operation Enduring Freedom) during a Taliban prisoner revolt at Qala-i-Jangi, an old fort outside Mazer e-Shariff, Northern Afghanistan. The fort had been converted into a prison holding area for Taliban prisoners. Spann coincidently had just discovered that Lindh, one of the captured Taliban prisoners, was an American while interrogating him in the courtyard of the holding area.

John Walker Lindh wasn't a terrorist in the truest sense of the word, and he wasn't the first young American to take up arms against fellow Americans, but he was among a very small group of "firsts." His actions gave America the first warning signs of change to come. As a result of Lindh's actions, Americans woke up to the possibility that young men and women who grew up in comfortable surroundings, enjoying all the safety and security America could offer, were capable of turning their backs on all that and embracing a culture that had as a goal the destruction of thousands of people, most often fellow Americans they had never met. For the first time, most Americans began to wonder, why and how.

Lindh wasn't a terrorist in the truest sense of the word additionally because Lindh didn't follow the traditional path into terrorism, the path we have seen emerge over and over again for the past couple of decades. Lindh fought with the Taliban, and the Taliban is considered a "regional" terrorist organization; however, the vast majority of its members at that time had never taken part in acts of terrorism, and during the time Lindh was with them, they were too busy fighting a semi-legitimate war against an organized enemy, to break away and conduct acts of terrorism. That of course has all changed with today's Taliban. John Walker Lindh just gave us an inkling of a change coming toward us, and he was among the first to do this (Figure 2.2).

Lindh was referred to as the "American Taliban" and, on occasion, the "American Terrorist." About the same time Lindh was in Afghanistan however, another emerged on the international scene and brought this same fear Lindh would bring to Americans to the entire world, the fear of random acts of terror that would kill innocents.

Ilich Ramirez Sanchez, born in Venezuela in 1949, grew up bullied by his fellow classmates because he was overweight. His schoolmates often referred to him as el Gordo (fat). As an adolescent, he began to work out heavily and do everything he could to change his physical appearance.

Figure 2.2 Qala-i-Jangi Fort Outside Mazer e-Shariff in Northern Afghanistan (Source: Author's personal photo).

21

He also decided to show the world that he was a man to be reckoned with. His first attempt to do this involved traveling to Beirut to join the Popular Front for the Liberation of Palestine (PFLP). This was two years after Lindh had left for Pakistan (for timeline purposes) (Figure 2.3).

It's fair to say that Sanchez wasn't the brightest bulb in the box. He had trouble talking his way in, pleading for acceptance, and even then, his fellow PFLP members were skeptical. He was given a couple of tests first.[4]

Figure 2.3 Ilich Ramirez Sanchez, aka "Carlos the Jackal."

His first test was to drive into town with a pistol provided by his handler, walk up to the front door of a man the organization wanted killed, knock on the door and shoot the man in the head as he opened the door. Sanchez did so. When the man came to the door, Sanchez raised the pistol to his head and pulled the trigger. His aim however was off and the bullet entered the left side of the man's head and traveled around the skull under the skin, exiting the back without ever penetrating the skull. The impact wasn't even enough to render the man unconscious, though it did understandably cause him some confusion. As the man stood there looking at Sanchez with a "what did you do that for" look on his face, Sanchez cocked the pistol and pulled the trigger again only to know that there were no more bullets in the gun. Realizing this, he dropped the gun and ran, returning to the handler.

"You gave me a gun with only one bullet," he complained.

"Yes, and you apparently didn't check it," came the reply along with a prompt request that Sanchez leave the premises. He didn't leave however. He begged for another chance.

"I'll do anything," he promised. "Just give me one more chance."

The handler relented and gave him another shot at membership in the organization. As it happened, there was a gathering of a group of political enemies of the PFLP to be held at a local hotel. Sanchez was given a satchel packed with explosives, shown how to activate it by pulling a cord and told to go to the hotel, open the front door, pull the cord and fling the satchel into the lobby where the meeting was being held.

Sanchez went to the hotel at the prescribed time, pulled the cord and threw the satchel through the door only to know that the door was a revolving one. As he threw the satchel, he pushed hard on the door to rotate it. The door did indeed rotate completely around bringing the satchel back around to where Sanchez was standing. He turned and ran, narrowly avoiding being blown up as the satchel exploded.

His pleas to be given one more chance almost failed, but he did indeed get one more assignment.

His handler Abu Sharif gave him the code name Carlos (he would later be referred to as The Jackal following the release of the Fredrick Forsyth's novel, "The Day of the Jackal," in 1971).

Soon the world would know of the exploits of the terrorist Carlos the Jackal, and as this knowledge came roughly the same time as the arrest of John Walker Lindh, America began to realize we were entering a period of time that would be impacted by acts of terrorism, and it was highly likely that many taking part in such actions would be our own sons and daughters.

23

WHY

The very first phrase human beings have a fairly clear understanding of, and the very first coupling of a string of words that we clearly understand, is "that's not fair." Human beings understand this phrase almost as early as they understand how to ask for food, and the idea that some things are unjust stays with us from that point forward. We never lose sight of this, and we just learn how to cope and accept to an extent.[5]

"Fairness" connotes balance, a state that humans the world over, throughout history, have sought and, once found, have struggled to maintain. Balance, "fairness," once achieved, allows us to progress. Native Americans hold spiritual ceremonies today, to allow individuals to achieve and maintain balance. Sigmund Freud used hypnosis in therapy to allow his patients to regress to a time of certain incidents that threw them out of balance and take steps (if only in their own mind) to achieve balance. Our present system or rule of law is designed to achieve balance, which again in essence is "righting wrongs." The only problem with this entire process is determining what throws things out of balance, and what it is going to take to reacquire balance. Fairness, in a nutshell, is in the eyes of the beholder, and this is never as evident as it is to combatants, especially those who embrace Islamism as opposed to moderates in the Islamic community.

Among terrorists one of the authors has interviewed, there is a highly refined and clearly understood concept of right and wrong that comes from their understanding of fairness. Of course, others take exception to their interpretation of events and their definition of fairness, but this is irrelevant and doesn't change the perceptions of those who are willing to act on it. This author had very slight success at changing some perceptions over time, but not enough to make a difference.

The most effective and committed terrorists believe fervently that the Islamic people (their people) have been victimized by a far superior group, and there's only one way to "right this wrong." Of course, the recruiters and handlers of those who commit terrorist acts are adept at using and exploiting this feeling, but the feeling that something just "isn't fair" has to be there to begin with.

Islamic extremist recruiters build a narrative for potential recruits that hold this message:

> You are a member of a huge family. You have brothers and sisters all over the world who love you and depend on you.

These brothers and sisters are being tortured and killed systematically by a force which is far superior, militarily.

If the appropriate recruit is selected, this message resonates and hits home. This message resonates especially with converts who are eager to prove their worth to their new-found religion and religious family. When people are recruited, radicalized and/or converted to a new religion, they often become extreme in their beliefs due to a desire to demonstrate their passion and convictions to other followers of the group/religion/ cult/extremist group. It is relatively easy for terrorist recruiters to target new converts and convince them to act as suicide bombers, carry out attacks or other such acts to "prove" their loyalty and commitment to the cause. Many people join cults, extremist groups, and become religious because they have overriding feelings of their life "not being fair" and have been searching for some greater meaning as to why events in their lives have taken place. This recruitment message of "life has not been fair to you and we can make it right" is one that works well with women who have experienced stifling home lives due to religious or cultural norms. Women, mainly young, modern women, who come from strict homes where they are not allowed to drive, go to school, choose a mate, listen to secular music or attend dances, often succumb to the terrorist's message of a new life and freedom from unfair/unjust conditions.

NOTES

1 Volkan, V. (1998). *Bloodlines: From ethnic pride to ethnic terrorism*, (p. 160). Westview Press.
2 Gurkha. (2020, December 10). In *Wikipedia*. https://en.wikipedia.org/wiki/ Gurkha.
3 Friedman, H. A. (n.d.). The chieu hoi program of Vietnam. *Psywarrior*. Retrieved May 15, 2020, from http://www.psywarrior.com/ChieuHoiProgram.html.
4 Ray, M. (n.d.). Carlos the Jackal. *Britannica*. Retrieved May 16, 2020, from https://www.britannica.com/biography/Carlos-the-Jackal.
5 Tabibnia, G. (2008, April 15). Are humans hardwired for fairness? *APS*. Retrieved May 16, 2020, from https://www.psychologicalscience.org/news/ releases/are-humans-hardwired-for-fairness.html.

3
Terrorist Landscape
Laying a Foundation

THE ENEMY

This text will to a great extent focus on slight, behind the scenes, nuanced anecdotal information about some of the most prolific terrorists and terror leaders the world has known to date. To begin with however, we will establish some fairly universal (universal in terms of terrorists and terror organizations) similarities shared by these individuals.

If you were to prioritize the enemies of virtually all Islamists and terror groups, westerners (Americans) would rate low on the list. Westerners are hated by Islamists mostly because they are emulated to various extents by the leaders and rulers of predominantly Muslim countries. They hate us because their leaders want to be like us and want their homelands to follow in the moderate steps of America and nations of the west.

Muslim leaders who try to "westernize" the culture of their people have generally provided the fuel for the fire that eventually became Al Qaeda, Al Qaeda in Iraq, ISIS, the Taliban (to an extent), Boko Haram and Al Shabaab. At the heart of this hatred for their nation's leadership is the simple mandate that "non-Muslim" feet can never tread sacred Muslim soil, especially in the holiest Muslim cities and locales. A foreigner even today, as a matter of fact, can never cross through Mecca in order to traverse to the opposite side of the city, as they are non-Muslim. In light of this, inviting Americans to Saudi or any other Islamic country, especially when those Americans are soldiers, is a disgrace among strict adherents to Wahhabism.

These west-embracing leaders have been seen by the Wahhabists and Salafists in their countries as turning away from Allah for the convenience of music videos and movie theaters and the opportunity to provide public education for young females. They are seen as "wanting to be American." The ire of the Islamists in these cases is ultimately kindled and directed toward America, Americans and westerners in general. The anger toward "west leaning national leaders and rulers," which fueled the formation of the most well-known terror groups, was felt strongly by Osama bin Laden, founder of Al Qaeda, against the Saudi royal family; by Ayman al-Zawahiri, bin Laden's second in command when he (bin Laden) lived, and current Al Qaeda leader, against the ruler of Egypt; by Abdullah Azam, one of the founders of Hamas, Al Qaeda, and Lashkar-e-Taiba (Lashkar was the first group to publicly behead a detainee, Wall Street Journal's Daniel Pearl), against the leaders of Palestine; and most fervently by Abu Musab al-Zarqawi (born Ahmad al-Khalayleh), founder of Al Qaeda in Iraq and ISIS, against the royal family of Jordan (it is recommended by the authors that these births be recorded on timeline).

The goal of the Islamist (fundamental hardline Islamic) groups is to return Islam to its unpolluted origins, using terrorism as a means to an end. Additionally of course, to complicate the social fabric of pre-dominantly Islamic nations and their peoples, there is a vast difference of opinion as to the desired state of Islam and the best way to achieve such desired state. The moderates do not see Islam as "polluted" by the western ideals they may choose to embrace. Also, as is the case with many Protestant and Catholic groups as well, there is a vast gulf between the fundamentalists, hardline and the moderate concepts of just what is Allah's (God's) will. In fairness, the moderate view is virtually never forced upon the will of the fundamentalists using violence, whereas such is SOP (standard operating procedure) with Islamists.

To encapsulate, the struggle, initially against the leaders of the Islamic nations from which these terror leaders come, can be easily and probably more understandably couched as a struggle between the hardliners, the Islamists and the moderates. And, just to make things more interesting, when boredom begins to settle in among these various groups, they are also known for turning on each other with the use of terrorism, if there is a question as to who is "more pure."

The vast majority of individual Muslims in these nations, while pious and devoted to Islam, are moderates in that, for instance, they can see no Islamic prohibition against education for all. Additionally, some western-type ideals or freedom of actions for women in their society are also seen as acceptable within the Islamic community. The Islamists, the Wahhabists and Salafists, conversely see all these individuals and their ideologues fueled and supported by the west-leaning leaders of these countries as, in many cases, the enemy.

Two individuals can be cited as most influential in the Islamism fundamentalist movements that spawned Al Qaeda, ISIS, Boko Haram and others. Abdul Wahhab, the founder of Wahhabism, and Sayyid Qutb, an Egyptian author, poet and educator and one of the leading members of the Muslim Brotherhood, were members of that rare brotherhood of "born leaders," and they were devout Islamists. They preached, wrote about and eventually led men into revolution designed to rid their nations (Sayyid Qutb was Egyptian and Wahhab was a Saudi) of the leadership in place at the time and return the Muslim world to its origins, the era of the Rashidun, as they interpreted it. They not only preached and urged resistance, but were adamant that those who stood in their way, including the leadership of their countries, should be killed. They were further successful in convincing their followers that it was their Islamic duty to fulfill this Jihad (struggle) and "kill the kafir or infidel" (Figure 3.1).

To be fair, the leaders they were fighting against, at least in the case of Qutb, were fairly brutal in their crackdown on these movements, and such actions always spur the enthusiasm of the resisters. The Egyptian government routinely imprisoned fundamentalists for handing out leaflets and even publicly humiliated and punished the females who chose to wear the Hijab in public. Sayyid Qutb was convicted of plotting to assassinate the President of Egypt Nasser and hanged in 1966. Both men however are revered by most terrorist leaders even today.

Most Islamist movements that spawned terror groups had their ideological origins in Saudi Arabia. Of course this was primarily a Sunni ideology, but the basics are revered by Shiite groups as well. Wahhabism, the predominant ideology among Saudi terror groups, was birthed in Saudi Arabia. Additionally, Sayyid Qutb, the religious leader regaled by most international terrorists (including bin Laden and Ayman al-Zawahiri to name a few), though not a Saudi, rather an Egyptian (he was hung in Egypt in 1966), was highly influenced by Wahhabist ideology from Saudi Arabia. Of course, we know that most of the 9/11 hijackers were Saudi. Throughout this study, do not lose sight of these influences on the broader international picture of terrorism. These two influences, Sayyid Qutb and Wahhabism, founded by Abdul Wahhab, are predominant influences in the groups we will examine, even, as stated, to an extent, the Shiite terror groups and Islamist terror groups based in other parts of the world.

Figure 3.1 Sayyid Qutb, Egyptian writer and much lauded figure among Sunni Wahhabists' terror organizations, hanged in 1966 for sedition activities[1].

Sayyid Qutb, the mentor of Ayman al-Zawahiri, for instance saw the world, and particularly his home Egypt, as divided into two competing states or ideologies: pure Islam and Jahiliyyah or a "dark time," essentially, the world before Mohammad. Qutb, a Salafist who was hung by Egypt in 1966 for his anti-government preaching, taught that Islam had to defeat the "near enemy" (the moderates among them) first and then the "far enemy," the west.

Getting back to the "enemies list" discussed earlier, at the top as discussed, would be "other Muslims," followed by Jews and westerners (America and America's allies). Of all the victims of acts of terrorism throughout the world, Muslims make up the vast majority. Most of this violence in the form of terrorism is carried out by Sunnis and targets the Shiite, who they see as acquiescent to the moderate ideology, among other things. Among much of the Sunni population, at least the population that make up the members of Al Qaeda, ISIS and the Taliban,

Shiites in most cases are more of an enemy than the Jews. The rationale dictates to an extent that "Islam cannot be cleansed and made pure, if the Shiites are not converted or eliminated." Sunni Muslim hardliners have historically blamed the Shiite for every setback ever experienced by Islam as a whole.[2]

Another common trait among terrorists and group leaders is the need to be seen as pious and religiously pure in their deeds, acting of and through Quranic authority. After all, the sects of Wahhabism and Salafism (who make up the majority of most terror groups) are considered the most pious and "purest" followers of Islam. The reader must keep in mind that Mohammad promised his followers a return to the greatness that was once Islam, if they strictly follow the teachings of Mohammad (by extension, instructions from Allah), and it is well-known among Muslims the world over that Muslims and the followers of Islam were once the most powerful people in the world. Among Islamists, that state of power and world domination is within reach and will come to fruition once the Caliphate is reestablished and/or the Mahdi (the 12th Imam) has returned. The Mahdi, 12th Imam, believed by Shiite to be infallible ruler of Islam, is said to have gone into occultation at the age of four. Occultation is a sort of suspended animation from which the 12th Imam will one day return.

To continue the purity narrative and its importance to fundamentalist Islam, however, strictly following the teachings of Mohammad, as they are interpreted by these individuals (interpretation of the teachings and instructions of Mohammad are at the heart of most conflict in Islam), is of utmost importance.

The glory and power of the Islamic world has seemed within reach and conversely extremely distant at times throughout history, and to the Islamists, this movement has always hinged on Muslim's adherence to the teachings of Mohammad as they interpret. Remember, according to their interpretation of the Quran and to an extent the Hadith (a collection of sayings – separate from the Quran of Mohammad amounting to guidance from Allah), Islam will be returned to glory as long as Muslims adhere to the commands of Allah.[2]

These commands are gleaned from the Quran and, just as biblical teachings, are often subject to wide interpretation. The interpretation most often held up by extremists, as guidance, is set forth through Sharia law. Additionally, most extremist Sunni Muslims, especially those who make up the followers of Al Qaeda, Islamic State and the Taliban (note: Islamic State and ISIS are often referred to as Daesh. The terms are pretty much interchangeable. In this text, we will refer to them as ISIS), see Shiite Muslims as apostates (non-believers) and primarily responsible for Islam's falling away from Allah.

As such, piety and validation by religious leaders are extremely important. Followers of Musab Zarqawi, leader of AQI (Al Qaeda in Iraq), while fully intending to be as brutal and callous as they possibly could, by actions such as public beheadings, burning opponents alive and sexually enslaving minors, among other atrocities, were quick to defer to their own personal traveling Mullah (anyone educated to some extent in Islamic theology) from whom they were confident they would get a thumbs up on even the most egregious or cruel actions toward their fellow human beings. The Mullahs, for the terrorists, are there to validate their (the terrorist leaders) sense of fairness, or right and wrong, and to validate their decisions as to what it will take to right wrongs.[3]

AQI fighters under Musab Zarqawi enslaved, raped and sexually tormented minors, mostly of the Yazidi people, as young as 12. They were quick to condone this by turning to their religious leaders who validated it as prescribed by the Quran. Under Quranic teachings, they would point out that enslaving or sexually violating these young girls is not only allowed but also required, as they are non-believers. Thus, as validated by their own personal Mullah, Quranic interpretation allowed making sex slaves out of 12-year-olds while carefully avoiding 11-year-olds as the Quran forbade this.

Most, if not all, terror group leaders keep their religious "go-to" people close and depend on them to give religious credence to their most heinous acts. Musab Zarqawi was taken down following a multi-year search, as a matter of fact, because he had summoned his personal Mullah to his hideout. American special forces had been surveilling the young religious scholar Zarqawi had adopted as his personal advisor, and simply followed him one day when he left with his entourage in somewhat of a hurry.[3]

In summation, they have a general hatred or resentment of the leaders in their own countries, due to embracing western ideals; the need to be seen as pious in all actions, however egregious; a similar ranking of enemy (prioritized enemies list); and finally, it is instructive to note that most of these terror leaders crossed paths frequently or before they became successful terror leaders. As we go through the more intimate details of these relationships, it is suffice to say at this point that they were not always of a like-mind in most areas. The one thing that did/ does always bind them however is the aforementioned "enemies list."

ISTISHHAD; SHAHADAT, THE MARTYR

When we think about terrorism or terrorist organizations, we generally, on some level, consider the associated aspect, which produces a level of terror. After all, a terrorist group is supposed to "terrorize." In consideration of this, we focus on the willingness of the group participants to martyr themselves, an act that is referred to as "istishhad." It is also referred to as "shahadat," the participant of which is referred to as "shahid."[4]

The first modern times recorded act of *shahadat* was in Lebanon in 1981. The *shahid* in this case was a Shiite, though Shiite terror groups have not been the most prolific users of the act. The use of suicide as a tool of war was introduced by the Palestinians, but it was perfected and made as common as the automatic weapon by the Sunni (to be exact Osama bin Laden's replacement as Al Qaeda leader, Ayman al-Zawahiri of Egypt). The Sunni terror groups which, by the way, make up the majority of terrorist organizations, however (Al Qaeda, ISIS, Taliban and most of the terror groups of the Islamic Maghreb are Sunni), have made the greatest use of *shahadat* throughout the years.

Since Islamic terror groups are so adamant that their actions be in accordance with divine guidance and instructions found in the Quran and the Hadith and/or, as in this case, actions taken by those closest to the leaders of the Rashidun Caliphate, how can such an action that is almost assured to kill the innocent as well as the combatant be sanctified and used today seemingly without a second thought?

As stated, the first use of such a tool as an act of terrorism was by Shiite in Lebanon. A suicide bomber detonated a vehicle with him at the wheel. In the past 5 years, there have been more than 2000 suicide attacks in 27 countries around the world, as stated, most committed by Sunni terror groups. That first one, however, back in 1981 in Lebanon was sanctioned and carried out by Shiite forces. How could they have deemed such an action within the will of Allah?

For the Shiite, the five most venerated religious figures in history are, of course, The Prophet Mohammad, his daughter Fatima, his son-in-law (and cousin and first convert to Islam) Ali and the two sons of Ali and Fatima, Mohammad's grandsons Hasan and Husayn. The annual Shiite religious celebration of Ashura recognizes these five but mostly Husayn.[2]

Why Husayn, to some extent even more so than Mohammad? The reason is because Husayn ibn Ali, who was slain by his enemy the Yazidi, is considered to have sacrificed himself in the battle of Karbala for the Shiite community that existed at that time and all the Shiite who would come thereafter. The fight at that time, just like most of the struggles in that period, was over who would lead Islam. The Yazidi (the term wasn't used then, but the Yazidi would have been considered Sunni Muslims, while Husayn of course was a blood descendent of Mohammad and would have been considered a Shiite) demanded that Husayn and his followers surrender and swear allegiance to the second Umayyad caliph, Yazid.[2]

Husayn refused and was eventually slain, decapitated, with his head displayed as a trophy of war. His followers too were slain, and their wives and children were taken into slavery. The actions of Yazid were seen as so abhorrent that they still today, especially during Ashura, hold the power to inflame Shiite observants of the occasion.

The actions of Husayn, at Karbala, offering up his life as a sacrifice to encourage Shiite Muslims from that day forward to resist enslavement and maintain their religious independence, were co-opted on that day in 1981 by the Hezbollah suicide bomber and his organization. They saw Husayn's actions as sanctified and blessed by Allah (which they very well may have been). They further saw any such acts they themselves may commit as modern-day *shahids*, as such, similarly sanctified and blessed. They did what religiously motivated zealots from many religious cultures around the world did, and still do; they pulled from the Holy record, in this case the religious history of Islam, what they wanted to find and interpreted it to support what they wanted it to support. *Shahids* from that day forward, whether Sunni (mostly Sunni as has been stated) or Shiite, simply picked up where the Shiite suicide member and his people in 1981 left off.

There were several, not so subtle, differences however in what Husayn did and what the *shahids* and their acts of *shahadat* do today. To begin, Husayn did not intend to sacrifice himself. As a matter of fact, if he could have avoided it, he probably would have. He even tried to negotiate with the Yazidis while still maintaining the rights of himself and his followers to pursue their religious goals and objectives in Islam. Jesus, as a matter of fact, did something similar. He prayed and asked God that "this cup pass from him. He of course caveated that request with the proclamation, "not my will but yours, be done."

The lesson from Husayn to those who would come after just may have been that martyring oneself should not be the first option. The lesson from Husayn and Jesus Christ, and the most important lesson however, the one which has escaped both Shiite and Sunni *shahids*, are that martyrs martyr themselves alone, not all those who happen to be around them at the time.

This is a key point.

THE SMALL WORLD OF TERRORISM

Before we get too far into this area, we'd like to give a quick tutorial on a process known in the intelligence community as "link analysis." Being able to construct a simple link analysis table and update it as you go along, just as the timeline, gives a new, valuable perspective to this subject.

A link analysis chart is nothing more than a visual, detailing who is connected to whom, and how such connections were established, and to an extent, how they are maintained. It is not a lot different from what you did in high school when you were a new freshman, socially determining who was who and who was with who, basically a pictorial "who's who" of terrorists.

You can get fancy with it, but this is not necessary. For instance, you can visually depict a good relationship as well as a bad one. You can signify who is superior to whom and in what way. You can also indicate secondary relationships, for example, A knows B and A knows C, and while B and C also know A, they don't know each other (these types of relationships are common in terror cells where it is important that few people in the cell know everyone involved) (Figure 3.2).

This section will point out some of the "chance" meetings and associations between leaders of these terror groups. I mention chance in quotes because it must be understood that even though some of these associations seem coincidental (as they are to a degree), the world of extremist Islam is truly a small world. Much of the ideology that has fostered the formation of Al Qaeda, ISIS, Al Shabaab and so on was gained from listening to speakers and teachers who were prominent Wahhabists or Salafists, so it is natural that they would have mentored, either directly or indirectly, the individuals who went on to be prominent leaders in the world of Islamic extremism. In many cases, several future terror leaders may have been in the "same class" in college, metaphorically speaking.

Osama bin Laden and Ayman al-Zawahiri, for instance, were both students at roughly the same time, and Abdullah Azam, co-founder of Al Qaeda and later a prominent leader in the organization along with bin Laden and Zawahiri (coincidently, by the way, it is highly likely that Zawahiri ordered the assassination of this same Azam), was a teacher/speaker/mentor to this same group of students. It's not clear whether they (bin Laden and Zawahiri) hung out together during the time they were learning from Azam, but given the nature of the teaching and their leanings, it would not have been unusual. As a matter of fact, it would

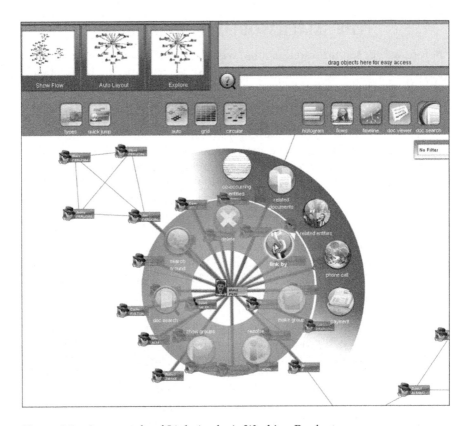

Figure 3.2 An example of Link Analysis Working Product.

have been highly likely since the groups of students during this period were more intimate in size. Of course, the three of them worked closely together later, in Pakistan, in support of the Mujahideen (Afghan freedom fighters battling the Russian occupation) fighting the Russians in Afghanistan.

Many cultures are prone to exaggerating the prowess of their heroes, and Afghans have taken the "exaggeration" process to great heights. The war against Russia was a fertile field for such stories, heroes and ex-aggerations. It was also a perfect time and place for the fraternity of future terrorist leadership and long-lasting friendships to gain a foothold. Of course, it was a perfect place for future antagonistic relationships to also gain a foothold. The only thing that mattered to any of these players of course, at this time, was defeating the infidel Russian invaders, and they were united in that effort. It is also likely that the current ideological framework in which age-old enemies can so easily unite for a common goal (such as battling the Jews) strengthened during that period. Many things happened during that decade-long war, which would have profoundly affected current events relating to international terrorism. Many future leaders of Islamic extremism, as well as those who would wage war against extremism, laid the foundation for their reputation during this period in Afghanistan. At that time and place however, they were all on the "same sheet of music" (Figure 3.3).

Ironically, the Mujahideen fighters (many if not most of whom later became members of the Taliban) were seen as heroes and freedom fighters, if you will, to the rest of the world. The music group Dire Straits even wrote a song, *Brothers in Arms*, that was rumored to have been about the Mujahideen fighters, though it was actually about the Falklands War.

While it is true that not all Mujahideen became members of the Taliban, the fact is that most of them (especially the Pashtun from the southern part of the country) did, and in actuality, all of the most prominent leaders of the Taliban had been Mujahideen. Osama bin Laden had even taken part in at least a single battle and distinguished himself to a degree, though he wasn't really a trained fighter.

When the Afghans began their long war to rid the country of the Russian invaders, many if not all Muslim nations issued a "call to arms" for its young men to travel to that country to assist. Of course bin Laden was already there, along with Zawahiri and Abdullah Azam, in Pakistan in an important support role. A young Mullah Mohammad Omar (future leader of the Taliban) was just another fighter in the ranks of the enlisted, and even Ahmad al-Khalayleh (Musab Zarqawi) received the call in his native Jordan and got in on the tail end of the war, arriving in country shortly before the Russians left[3,5] (Figure 3.4).

This was a time and place for many future terror leaders to meet and become inspired to Jihad. Bin Laden recruited thousands of young Arabs (often referred to as Afghan Arabs) from his native Saudi Arabia, to come to the fight. Anecdotally, the Arabs and the Afghans didn't get along. The Arabs, from a much wealthier country, were seen as aloof and self-righteous by the Taliban, many of whom spent months in the mountains without proper shoes on their feet. The Arabs also frowned upon many of the Afghan religious practices, such as decorating graves, and often imposed their form of Wahhabism on their hosts.

(a)

(b)

(c)

Figure 3.3 Early photos of (a) bin Laden, (b) Abdullah Azam and (c) Ayman al-Zawahiri all probably taken during the period of time when the foundational organization for Al Qaeda was formed in Pakistan.

Figure 3.4 Mullah Mohammad Omar, Taliban Supreme Commander.[6]

Three of the most influential figures during the war against Russian occupation were bin Laden, Ayman al-Zawahiri and Abdullah Azam. These individuals were/are important because they were instrumental in the formation of Al Qaeda, arguably the "mother of terror organizations."

As stated earlier, bin Laden took part in one or more battles when they occurred close to a training camp he had set up across the border in eastern Afghanistan, but he mostly maintained a support structure from inside Pakistan, recruiting and facilitating travel for volunteers and funneling cash to the fighters. Zawahiri (who had along with bin Laden studied under Abdullah Azam) became close to bin Laden in Pakistan during the war. Zawahiri was a physician and had journeyed to Pakistan to assist, treating the wounded Afghan fighters who could make it there.

There, he met and became an advisor for bin Laden (later taking over Al Qaeda after bin Laden's death at the hands of US Navy SEALs in 2011).

Many analysts believe that Zawahiri was jealous of Azam's influence over bin Laden. Ironically, Azam was killed along with two of his sons in 1989, by a suicide bomber on a motorcycle, and though it was never proven, analysts believe the incident was set up and coordinated by Zawahiri.

In short, the "small world" of organized Islamic extremism and the men who were instrumental in it (though the ideology began and gained prominence with the birth of Wahhabism in the 16th century) has its origins then and there. Afghanistan, for all practical purposes, during that time was jihadism's "Hole in the Wall" (a reference to the *Hole in the Wall* pass in Johnson County Wyoming, a hideout and refuge for gangs of robbers and cutthroats in the old American west).

NOTES

1 Britannica. (n.d.). Muslim brotherhood. *Britannica*. Retrieved May 16, 2020, from https://www.britannica.com/topic/Muslim-Brotherhood.
2 Nasr, V. (2006). *The Shia revival: How conflicts within Islam will shape the future.* W. W. Norton and Company Publishers.
3 Warrick, J. (2015). *Black flags: The rise of ISIS*. Regan Arts.
4 Istishhad. (n.d.). In *Wikipedia*. Retrieved May 19, 2020, from https://en. wikipedia.org/wiki/Istishhad.
5 Rashid, A. (2010). *Taliban*. Yale University Press.
6 Mohammed Omar. (n.d.). In *Wikipedia*. https://en.wikipedia.org/wiki/ Mohammed_Omar.

4

How bin Laden Rose to Fame
A Historical Perspective

OSAMA BIN LADEN AND THE BASE (AL QAEDA)

To understand the type of Islamic extremism that manifests itself in the form of terrorism and the world of bin Laden, Musab Zarqawi and Zawahiri, it is important to understand Wahhabism. To understand Wahhabism, it is important to understand the origins and growth of Islam itself. As there are a multitude of volumes available about the Prophet Mohammad and the birth and development of Islam, not to mention the Quran itself, we will not go far into the history, but there are some aspects of this era that have a direct connection to the rise of some of the most prolific terrorists, and terror organizations, that should be discussed in order to provide a clearer understanding of motives and operational strategies of these individuals and groups.

As stated earlier, this text will use the things we (all of us) know to help us understand the things we do not. For instance, much of the revelations, as interpreted and reported in the Quran, by the Prophet Mohammad parallel Christian teachings as well as some teachings of Judaism. One in particular led to the first real conflict between The Prophet and the non-believing, or yet to be converted, Arabs, mostly of the upper socioeconomic class.

Mohammad, much like Jesus, taught and advocated for a more even distribution of wealth, and rich folks didn't appreciate this. At that time, among the Quraysh (Mohammad was a member of the Banu Hashim clan of the Quraysh), many men had become wealthy, trading in the region, and they didn't necessarily appreciate someone gaining prominence by advocating that they give half their wealth to the poor. It took Mohammad around 30 years to begin to gain some inroads among this group.

It also took him disavowing his own clan, the Quraysh, an act that was horrendous in the culture at this time, and moving with a group of followers to Mecca in order to escape danger to himself and his followers. In short, people didn't like his teachings and the fact that he was gaining in prominence and wanted to not only kill him but wipe out his followers. This hatred of Mohammad may be easily understood when considering the hatred of Jesus by the Jewish leaders, upon whose "turf" Jesus was trampling. As a matter of fact, though legend is slightly murky, Mohammad was poisoned in an act orchestrated by one or more of his many enemies.

It is important to view Islam, the Prophet Mohammad and events that occurred as Islam was developing in terms of the time and the location. It is also important to consider the difference in age between Christianity and Islam. Christians had been worshiping Jesus over 600 years when The Prophet Mohammad received his first revelation from God.

Life in this part of the world at that time was difficult, to put it mildly. Most of the tribes had a long history of warring with each other, and the vendettas and family feuds that existed were of principal consideration. Violence was common, and survival often depended on it.[1]

When Mohammad led his people to settle in Medina to escape persecution, he saw this as their only means of survival, conducting raiding parties on the caravans of wealthy merchants, acts in which injuries and deaths occurred. Today, as the Quranic texts are often twisted and interpreted in such a way so as to support acts of terrorism, some terror leaders and their supporters refer to this period as the Prophet Mohammad's acquiescence to the use of violence to achieve an end.[1]

To give this interpretation more credence, powerful Islamic leader and founder of the Islamic doctrine of Wahhabism, Muhammad ibn Abd al-Wahhab advocated violence as a useful tool to be used often. Founded in early 1700s, the doctrine took hold and recruited the father of the Saudi royal family Muhammad Bin Saud. It was later adopted by a young Osama bin Laden and most of the terrorist leaders who followed him.

ORIGIN OF THE SUNNI–SHIITE SPLIT

One of the most impacting processes in the development of Islam and later development and rise of so many terrorist groups was the original doctrinal split that set up the doctrines of Sunni Islam and Shiite Islam. This doctrinal split has a great deal of impact on our study of terror groups and terror leaders, so we will devote this section of the text on examining the background.

Today, most people can provide a general idea of the differences between these two doctrines, but few are knowledgeable of the actual events that led to this. As the hatred between these two ideologies, which exists to a degree even today, has so much impact on the rise of Islamic extremism and Islamic violence, it is important to examine as much as possible what happened and why.

First, try to envision the world as it existed at the time Mohammad was introducing Islam to the Arabs. Though it may sound trite, you must understand that Arabs were not always rich. Many young people today think the Arabs were always a wealthy, carefree people, but the opposite is true for this period and for that matter it was not until the early 1900s that oil was beginning to have an impact on the nation.

Arabs are still, to a great extent, a tribal people. As such, leadership of groups of people, whether nomadic or more stationary, was of utmost importance. When a leader got too old to lead or died, a great deal of thought went into his successor. When Mohammad died, the question of who was to become the new leader of the Islamic world was considered in a similar manner, but "doing it right," as all Arabs knew, was much more important. This was magnified additionally by the fact that Islam had become, in the short period between Mohammad's first revelation to the people, 610 AD to his death in 632 AD, a solidly grounded religion, and the selection of a new leader was of unbelievable importance.[2]

In most cases, a normal leader was selected based on his wisdom or maybe his experience or maybe even his wealth or property. In this case, the people looked at those who were closest to Mohammad in his life, and or those to whom he was tied by blood. Some believed that divine wisdom and prophetic attributes ran in the family, while others saw this as interesting but not necessarily all-encompassing.

Additionally, as Mohammad had led his people on several military operations and raids on caravans coursing through the area, he wasn't just a spiritual leader; he was a military strategist to a degree as well.

Initially, this divide wasn't the great gulf we know of today. It was more of a simple philosophical difference of opinion. Therefore, when the majority of decision-makers decided on Abu Bakr, father-in-law of Mohammad (an associate, rather than blood line) as the first Caliph (successor of Mohammad), there was no uproar of disagreement. Of significance additionally is the fact that in this time, the Arab culture was in large part one of settling differences with violence. As a result, the first four leaders of Islam (widely accepted, as they were closest to Mohammad, the most knowledgeable therefore, most venerated of Islamic leaders) did not die of natural causes.

It is important to note here that as stated, of all the successive leaders of Islam, the first four are most venerated as they were the closest in actual physical connection to Mohammad and considered to have the only real firsthand knowledge of Mohammad himself and of the direction and decisions Mohammad would have made reference Islam.[3] These four are known as the Rashidun or "Rightly Guided Ones." In a way, these four are synonymous with the disciples of Jesus because they knew personally, and actually had conversations with, Mohammad. Again, the terms Sunni and Shiite did not exist at this time. Abu Bakr may have died of illness, but many scholars of Islam assert it is possible (some say likely) that he was poisoned (as mentioned previously in the text). He reigned as leader of Islam for two years. He was succeeded by Umar, also father-in-law of Mohammad (Mohammad had four wives, the maximum a Muslim was allowed to have), who ruled for two years as well and murdered by Persian prisoner of war while in prostration in prayer. The third leader, Uthman, a member of the Umayyad family, an associate of Mohammad and also not bloodline, lasted 12 years.

It could be said that Uthman is responsible for orchestrating the split between Sunni and Shiite, though at first, it wasn't a split over the bloodline of the leader. Uthman was the first example in Islam of rule by "who you know rather than what you know." Uthman had a tendency to put favored friends and associates in all the places of power where profit could be made. This angered a large segment of Muslims who launched a revolt against the Islamic rule of Uthman, not unlike all the revolts against Islamic leadership in later generations, which gave rise to the likes of bin Laden, Zawahiri and Zarqawi. Many of the most disgruntled Muslims leading the revolt were soldiers. At the height of their anger, they went to Uthman's home demanding change and ended up killing him in the process.[3]

Those in revolt referred to themselves as Kharijites (Shiite e-Ali, partisans of Ali) and, as might be supposed, were the first Shiite.[3] They also instituted the first Jihad against leadership, insisting that the ruler of Muslims not be among the most powerful but among the most committed. They pressed for and eventually achieved rule of Islam by Mohammad's son-in-law Ali. Now, the fact that Ali had married Mohammad's daughter Fatima didn't make him bloodline, but in addition to son-in-law, he was also Mohammed's cousin as well as the first male convert to Islam, after Mohammad of course (When trying to keep track of all these players, your linear timelines can become a bit tangled. Use of the timeline again can help keep the tangles manageable in your mind.).

The Kharijites expected Ali being placed in leadership primarily because of them, to vehemently oppose those rulers and men in power placed there through a system of nepotism and cronyism from their perspective, but Ali struck a more conciliatory tone. This is a good example of politics at work even at this early stage. As often happens today, those who backed Ali to an extent felt slighted because of his reticence to use violence.

One of them who'd been placed in a position of power by Uthman was a man by the name of Muawiya. Muawiya was a member of the Umayyad family and a close friend of Uthman. As may be expected, he felt that he should have been the successor to Uthman, rather than Ali.

In a tone of conciliation and an attempt to ease tensions among Muslims, Ali met with Muawiya to make some sort of compromise. This attempt further stoked the "anti-Uthman" passions of the Kharijites who likely felt betrayed by the man they'd backed for the first "bloodline" Caliph (in terms of Shiite ideology, Ali was actually the first Imam; "Imam" being the principal term for a supreme Shiite leader, preferred over Caliph).

A seemingly strange thing occurred about this time. Ali was under a lot of pressure from his followers to get to the bottom of the assassination of Uthman. This pressure was coming primarily from Muawiya, but he was also being pressured by Mohammad's favorite wife Aisha.[3]

Muawiya, with an army, refused to pledge allegiance to Ali and decided instead to attack him and his followers. Ali was victorious in this battle but launched the aforementioned effort to ameliorate the situation and bring peace to Islam by uniting opposing forces. The Kharijites opposed the idea of reconciliation and, bitter over comrades who had been killed in battle with Muawiya, assassinated Ali.[1]

Continuing the bloodline leadership, Ali's death by assassination cleared the way for his son Hasan (Ali's marriage to Fatima, Mohammad's daughter provided him two sons, Hasan and Husayn) to take over. At this stage in the progression of Islam, two bloodline leaders and successors to Mohammad (Shiite) had been in control, Ali and his son Hasan. Hasan, however, apparently wanted nothing to do with leadership, took a bribe from Muawiya and retired to Medina, paving the way for Muawiya and his followers to take the reins.

Muawiya took leadership and control of Islam and passed it to his son Yazid, upon his death. The Islamic community was divided once again, some supporting Yazid and others pledging allegiance to Husayn, Ali's other son. Husayn, unlike Hasan, embraced the idea of leading the Islamic people and, as such, when demanded he do so, refused to pledge allegiance to or accept the legitimacy of Yazid as the leader of Islam, setting the stage for a civil conflict in the Islamic community.

> *Author's Note: Okay readers/students, just checking in with you here; you still with me? These relationships and number of people involved can become confusing, but stay the course, it will all make sense. It is important that you have a grasp of this because these issues still impact the actions of various Islamic extremist terror organizations even today.*

Husayn and his followers, while journeying to Kufa as a result of a letter from the people there asking his help and pledging allegiance to him, were set upon by Yazid's army near Karbala where he was killed along with most of his family including his six-month-old son (this event and this location, Karbala, are of great importance to the Islamic Shiite community even today). This marked the beginning of the real split between Sunni and Shiite Muslims, a split that is almost as virulent and violent today as it was in 680.

As stated in the initial part of this text, we want to provide the reader some contextual data that will allow them to more accurately understand the corresponding Islamic event, belief, ideology or, in this case, situation. It's difficult however to point out a similar cultural or racial divide in order to provide the reader with some comparable feeling of separation, feelings of animosity or even hatred toward another group. It is very important however that the readers have some concept of the vast gulf that existed at this time and still exists to a great extent today, between Sunni and Shiite Muslims. This gulf after all has contributed to thousands of deaths on both sides and, as is the case in most instances of racial or religious animosity and hatred, is based on perceptions, and as we know, perceptions are neither wrong nor right, they just are what they are.

We simply need to understand them to the extent possible.

Today, the Muslim population worldwide is approximately 85% Sunni and 15% Shiite. Saudi Arabia is the center of Sunni Islam, and Iran is populated predominately by Shiite. In most Islamic conflicts, Iran and Saudi fall on opposing sides, regardless of the nature of the conflict.[3]

At the heart of the dispute, however, even today is contention over the rightful leadership of Islam, between Sunni and Shiite.

The best understandable analogy we can offer is the differences that have existed between blacks and whites throughout history. As is the case with this particular racial divide, these differences initially grew very fast and became very vast. As time passed in most mixed-race communities, the divide between races somewhat lessened, though it flares now and then. We are currently seeing a great racial divide among numerous races that extends not just to the United States, but in a multitude of countries throughout the world with weekly attacks inspired by racial bias and hate. At the time of writing this book, the Jewish community within the United States has seen a record number of attacks, numbering over 2000 attacks in 2019 alone.[4]

The differences between Sunni and Shiite followed a similar pattern, though they obviously are not based on race. The difference probably began in earnest over the way Husayn was martyred. His death at the hands of Muawiya and his followers at Karbala, and the events surrounding it are a point of annual recognition in Shiite communities today in the Ashura commemoration. On that day, Shiite recognize the five most venerated religious figures in Shiite Islam, Mohammad, Ali, Fatima (Mohammad's daughter, wife of Ali, and mother to Husayn and Hasan), Husayn and Hasan. This is also a day for the remembrance of the martyrdom of Husayn. The events on the day of Ashura are also obviously a time for concern for security forces since there is often an escalation of conflict and violence between Shiite and Sunni. Imam Husayn was a martyr, but he was also a hero for the Shiite, and they blame the Sunni for his death. That blame and animosity contributes to various degrees of violence between these two ideologies but, as stated, is often escalated on the Day of Ashura.

The only difference between the analogy of mixed-race communities and the Sunni/Shiite ideological differences is the extent to which the violence between these groups has risen from time to time. Musab Zarqawi, whom we will discuss in Chapter 9 in this text and the terror leader who formed Al Qaeda in Iraq (later the beginning stages of ISIS), declared war on Shiites in Iraq, slaughtering thousands.

There is a connection with the animosity between Sunni and Shiite Muslims, and international and regional terrorism itself. Stated earlier in this text, the principal enemy of Islamic extremists is other Muslim. The "other Muslims" is most often exemplified by violence between Sunni and Shiite, though it would be described as an attempt by the "pure" Muslims to eradicate the "impure" (*kufr*, or infidel, disbeliever) Muslims among them. The fact is, to the Sunni extremist, the Shiite are the *kufr*, and to an extent, the opposite is also true. "Purity" in this sense is definitely in the eyes of the beholder.

There are terrorist groups that are predominantly Shiite (Hezbollah is most well-known), but the majority of terror organizations in the world today are Sunni.[5] Sunni terrorist groups adopted and misinterpreted for their own purposes the term *shahadat* (martyrdom), the fourth struggle in Islam. The Quran venerates the martyr who commits *shahadat* in the name of Allah. "When the first drop of blood comes out of his body, all his sins are pardoned" is one among a number of attractive inducements to *shahadat*.

The misinterpretation applied for their own purposes, by "initially" Sunni Muslim terror groups, comes in twisting the objective of the *shahid* (one who commits *shahadat*). Most Quranic scholars describe the act of *shahadat* as sacrificing oneself, not "oneself and every other (self) in the vicinity" of the act, which happens in most incidents of terror-inspired suicide (if you prefer martyrdom or *shahadat*). Sunni terror group leaders and recruiters are adept at inducing the "rewards of shahadat," but most Islamic scholars refute their interpretation. To be fair, Shiite terrorist groups, though slow to embrace the practice, are known to use it as well.

All in all, however, in summation of this section, it is safe to say the early years of Islam were characterized by conflict, warring and assassinations.

OVERARCHING PHILOSOPHIES

When organizations that would one day morph into terror groups began forming and the bubbles of anarchy and revolt began surfacing, there were a couple of different philosophies that would have to meld into one, in order for real progress to be made in the Middle East. Whether, these "battling philosophies" ever successfully blended into one objective are still disputed and depend on what questions you ask. Bin Laden and Zarqawi, for instance, disagreed vehemently over the use of women and children as

48

shahids (martyrs, suicide bombers) and the use of terroristic violence against other Muslims. Bin Laden was opposed to it but not necessarily "benevolently" in his intentions. He wanted to move slowly to unite all Muslims in support of the Caliphate. Zarqawi, on the other hand, wanted an apocalyptic burst of violent jihad (struggle), resulting in the emergence of the Caliphate and him as the Caliph, and he didn't care how many Muslims died to get it done. As a matter of fact, he saw the way to accomplish this lofty goal as igniting a war between Sunni and Shiite, which he did.[6]

The origins of this conflict however go far back in history. We examine it here because at some point, the use of women and children as suicide bombers emerged as a religiously sanctioned process and is still used today. This "emergence" was to a great degree controlled by the aforementioned conflict.

In the early 1990s, several "pan Arabic" groups began to flourish and gain momentum. Pan Arabism is a movement that seeks to unite Muslim countries in Northern Africa and Western Asia under one flag, led by Saudi Arabia and the Saudi royal family.[7] It is not necessarily a negative concept and, as a matter of fact, is a goal of many nations and cultures. In order to accomplish this goal however, one nation or one culture or sect (e.g., Sunni or Shiite) cannot be seen to dominate others and can definitely not be seen to eradicate others. Such a nationalistic movement, in order to be successful, must be supported by peoples from all nations, cultures and sects involved. The term itself exemplifies unification within the particular culture.

Leaders like Osama bin Laden, though they operated from a standpoint of hatred of the west to a great degree, were more embracing of such nationalism. As such, they were slow to buy into practices such as using women and children as suicide bombers. This later became a point of contention between Al Qaeda and ISIS as ISIS routinely targeted women to recruit and radicalize. Additionally, bin Laden was offended by much of Zarqawi and Zarqawi's associates brutalizing and sexually exploiting children and young women. Bin Laden was particularly incensed when Zarqawi, once settled in Northern Iraq, took a 13-year-old wife.

Bin Laden was by no means acting out of benevolence. He was concerned that his goal of uniting Muslims within the Caliphate would be inhibited by such actions. Leaders like Zarqawi, on the other hand, were "good" with the uniting aspect of nationalism, but they were equally intent on settling old grudges or wiping out Muslims and Islamic leaders with whom they saw as anathemas to their beliefs, and as stated, Zarqawi and his followers, not unlike many other terror groups, hated

Shiite Muslims and considered them apostates, worthy of annihilation. When Zarqawi was questioned, on the few instances where he was in custody of the Jordanian Mukabarat and confronted about the religious implications of killing women and children, he would respond that "it is not only accepted to kill apostates, it is required by Allah."

PAVING THE WAY FOR A TERRORIST; THE RISE OF OSAMA BIN LADEN: FIRST YOU HAVE TO HATE

Of all the "unknowns, and semi-knowns" in the study of terrorism, and they are "legion," one thing that is undisputed is that the real, active practicing and operational terrorists literally hate the "west," in particular America. The most common expression, or description of America, among these individuals is that "America is evil." Evil is never defined, but the implication is normally that America is decadent and that decadence in and of itself makes America evil.

On a related note, it is eye-opening that Muslims in this part of the world hate various groups (Sunnis hate Shiites, Muslims hate Jews and Americans), there's never a clear easily enunciated cause of such hate. This is fairly common with many groups who hate others, but in light of the fact that the hatred practiced by Islamists is often manifested through acts of terrorism, it is worth taking the time to consider the basis of the hate, if one can be found. When you ask a Sunni why they hate the Shiite, and vice versa, the response is generally vague.

People don't hate others simply because of who they are; they hate others because it is assumed that the "others" are taking something away from them or depriving them of a way of life that is vital to them. Sunnis who harbor hate for Shiites and vice versa (it goes without saying that not all Sunni or Shiite hate the other group, though it is more common than in other parts of the world) have been taught that everything bad that happens to Islam is caused by the Sunni or Shiite, depending on who you ask. This too is always vague.[3]

Once again, however, the hatred is palpable, profound and pervasive among this most committed class of terrorist. This is important in itself, because of the intensity of the feeling. Most adversaries in wars and conflicts, historically, have harbored a degree of hatred for their enemy. This (Islamist-based) hatred however is unusual for many reasons including its intensity. As a matter of fact, even though feelings approximating these exist in all adversarial situations that have historically produced armed conflict, there are many situations (some would say it is even common) where a grudging respect develops between enemies. No such thing is even imagined in the terrorist's resentment and hatred, especially for the west, predominantly America. This intensity of feeling is in itself worth examining to the extent possible.

As stated earlier, this text will use the "known" to try and understand the "unknown." As such we will examine some of the underlying cultural practices that have an effect on human growth and development in the Islamic community and try to see them in the context of normal human development in American communities. In doing so, we will compare the development and cultural norms of young men growing up in a western, predominantly Christian culture, to the development of young men growing up in a much more religiously restrictive society, keeping in mind that human beings are "human beings" and develop in much the same way, both physically and emotionally.

In a society like America as well as most European countries, interaction between sexes is encouraged to a degree, among young people, precisely because such controlled, supervised and guided interaction leads to a healthy relationship between sexes and a healthy sexual awareness in both males and females. Denying this "controlled interaction" in young people who are approaching the stage of human growth and development, where sexual awareness is predominant, research indicates, often produces skewed feelings of oneself and one's peers of both sexes.[8]

Back to the mixing of the sexes, and any related hatred for the west, it must be understood that even today Saudi Arabia is a highly controlled environment in terms of religious restrictions and the requirement for conformity. Women who go unveiled still today risk chastisement and/or outright punishment by the religious police, even though in the Prophet Mohammad's time, women were not required to cover their faces.

For Islamists, Saudi has always been "the chosen place," populated by the "chosen people," and they follow the Quran as their constitution. The irony is that as the Saudi royal family, going all the way back to one of its principal founders, Abdul Aziz ibn Saud, has always embraced the fundamentalists (Islamists) among them, often for purely political reasons, and has always allowed the fundamentalists to interpret the Quran, their ipso facto constitution, and all their attempts to modernize and to bring freedoms and luxuries to their people have met with severe resistance by these same fundamentalists, much of which has led to instances of terrorism in the pursuit of resistance and the pursuit of a "pure" Islamic society. Osama bin Laden himself was the target of an assassination attempt at a mosque in Saudi Arabia by a group of fundamentalists who determined he wasn't radical enough.

In highly controlled Islamic cultures, such as Saudi Arabia, in the name of religion (this is magnified among strongly fundamental communities), young people are denied many things seen as anti-Islamic, most impacting, a healthy interaction between the sexes. Such a controlled environment, just when young people are most curious and most in need of some understanding of the opposite sex, is highly problematic from a standpoint of normal human growth and development. In far too many occasions, it has serious consequences.

While there is little evidence of increased instances of homosexuality among young males in Islamic communities, there is evidence of sexual acting out and sexual domination among males associated with terrorist groups. The more violent the terrorist activity, the more prevalent the sexual domination of male counterparts is.

Musab Zarqawi, considered the founder of the current Islamic State movement, was known to demonstrate his power and prowess in such a way. In many instances in these environments, sexual interaction between males, though considered sinful (*haram*), is not seen as carrying the same religious condemnation as even the slightest interaction with females. While we are on the topic of sexual assault committed by extremely strict adherents of Islam, let's examine how these individuals can profess to living their lives according to the will of Allah and yet justify sexual assault on another human being.

The answer is simple and abhorrent: The individuals they choose to violate are seen as "less than human" in the eyes of their jihadist attackers. They are not seen as people of God, and as such, the laws of the Quran do not apply to them. Men and women alike that are unbelievers are stomped on by jihadists and their actions are justified, according to them, because they are not "children of God." The women that were taken captive by ISIS were generally of a minority sect that practiced a different religion (Yazidis, primarily). These women were made into sexual slaves by the men within the terrorist group (ISIS in this example), and this is not frowned upon because the mindset among extremists is that this is "what these women deserve" for their defiance of Allah.

Women are often seen as expendable to Islamic extremists, especially those that do not adhere to Sharia law or the strict rules that various terror groups impose. A recent example of the brutality against women by ISIS is the bombing of a maternity ward in a hospital in Afghanistan. This attack that took place in Kabul that killed 16 mothers, nurses and newborn babies. Masked gunmen stormed the hospital, with the specific intent of targeting the maternity ward, and brutally and heartlessly went from room to room, firing bullets at helpless newborn babies and their terrified mothers.[9]

As of the writing of this book, no terrorist group claimed credit to this attack. The authors have no doubt that by the time this book goes to publication, it will come to light who is responsible for such a horrendous crime. Whoever is determined to be behind such an attack is already showing their hand. They are showing that they have zero regard for the sanctity of life and that there are no "innocent" victims in their minds when it comes to their twisted sense of what is right and wrong, and what they believe is justified by Allah against the so-called apostate. Considering all this and the fact that many of the most successful terror leaders visited the west, including America, and those who did not were highly influenced by individuals who did, one has to wonder how the exposure to such a culture of freedom affected them.

Almost all these men, including bin Laden, returned preaching of the moral depravity and decadence of the American society, but how did they themselves respond to such environments, and what was the lasting effect of such on them personally? As we said in the initial portions of this text, we will compare the known with the unknown in order to make plausible conjectures.

Keeping in mind that one of the authors of this text is also a psychologist, this comparison is potentially arguable, but not very difficult to assess, based on a simple knowledge of human emotions and human growth and development including responses to such interactions.

For instance, we know that in many cases of highly emotional, negative reactions to homosexuality, by heterosexuals, the emotion is often as much fear-based as it is based on simple interpretations of morality. Simplistically, vast amounts of research indicate that many heterosexual males' hatred of homosexuals is due to some fear of repressed homosexual desires. These repressed desires, as normal as they may be, often lead to hate for the object seen as triggering them. So, just as the young heterosexual male in American culture may fear and abhor their own sexual curiosity, and place all the blame for this dichotomy of feelings on the homosexuals with whom they come into daily contact, the young Muslim male having grown up in such a sexually restrictive culture may abhor the feelings aroused within them by a permissive culture such as that in America (they may target these feelings of abhorrence especially against American women, who they see as scantily dressed and disgustingly promiscuous), and hate and blame America all the more for feelings they cannot rationalize. Going back to the introduction of this section, why the hatred of America and the west is so easily maintained and so often used in recruitment processes, and simple logic will support how the foundation for such reasoning is based upon young people growing up under such repression.

When these men, many of whom visit the United States at an early age (and these very normal and very "human" desires manifest themselves), see their emotions as repulsive to their sense of morals, they may blame the United States. The more their human nature encourages them to "desire" that which is "haram," the more they are repulsed at their own desire and the more they blame and hate America for it. Though hatred of America among Muslim fundamentalists cannot be solely attributed to such logic, it cannot be denied that a desire for the decadence they perceive as "American" and therefore anti-Islamic may easily contribute to such hatred.

The desire they experience is abhorrent to them, and human nature dictates that they must seek others to blame, something or someone outside themselves. Again, as the heterosexual who may experience some uncomfortable thoughts often blames the homosexual, and the Islamic fundamentalist, under similar circumstances, blames America. We also see this in some highly fundamentalist Islamic societies where women are blamed for all "impure" thoughts males may experience. As such the woman must be completely covered in order that such desires, which are seen as contrary to Islamic teachings, will be controlled or eliminated. Women must abstain from wearing high heels because the tapping sounds that such heels make on the floor, while walking, are considered titillating to the male, and the arousal and distraction are considered overwhelming. Such "overwhelming desire" is also considered triggered by the sight of women's flowing hair (thus the mandatory covering of women's hair), and ultimately, all such distractions for men are seen as distracting them from their worship of, and total dedication to, Allah. The fundamentalist sees American decadence and their own aroused carnal nature, and they fear and loath this. It is not difficult to see how such a chain of observations and emotions can easily lead to, and maximize, the "hate" for the west and for America.

NOTES

1 Trofimov, Y. (2008). *The siege of Mecca: The forgotten uprising in Islam's holiest shrine and the birth of al-Qaeda.* Anchor Publishing.
2 Armstrong, K. (2002). *Islam: A short history.* Modern Library Chronicles.
3 Nasr, V. (2006). *The Shia revival: How conflicts within Islam will shape the future.* W. W. Norton and Company Publishers.
4 Statista Research Department. (2020). Number of anti-semitic incidents in the United States from 2008 to 2019. *Statista.* https://www.statista.com/statistics/816732/number-of-anti-semitic-incident-in-the-us/.
5 Weiss, M. (2015). *ISIS: Inside the army of terror.* Phaidon Publishers.
6 Warrick, J. (2015). *Black flags: The rise of ISIS.* Regan Arts.
7 Pan-Arabism. (n.d.). In *Wikipedia.* Retrieved May 21, 2020, from https://en.wikipedia.org/wiki/Pan-Arabism.
8 Bankroft, J. (2009). *Human sexuality and its problems* (3rd ed.). Churchill Livingston.
9 Akrami, M., Frogh, W., & Seraj, M. (2020, May 16). OPINION: We shouldn't have to ask that babies and mothers not be killed. Yet we must. *NPR.* https://www.npr.org/sections/goatsandsoda/2020/05/16/856999032/opinion-mothers-and-infants-should-not-be-a-tar get-in-afghanistan-s-path-to-peac.

5

A Closer Look at bin Laden

THE BIN LADEN FAMILY STRUCTURE

It is worth noting that Osama bin Laden was one of the few terrorists who did not change his name, effectively adopting the name of an admired martyr, leader from history, or the name of their chosen homeland (a habit of most young men who embrace Islamism and join jihadist terror organizations). Most terror leaders went through this name change.

Abu Bakr al-Baghdadi, the Islamic State leader killed by American Special Operations teams in 2019, was born Ibrahim Awwad Ibrahim al-Badri. Abu Musab al-Zarqawi, the founder and first leader of modern ISIS, was born Ahmad al-Khalayleh in Jordan. Abu Bakr took the name of the first leader of Islam following the death of the Prophet Mohammad. The (al-) means from, thus Abu Bakr al-Baghdadi (from Baghdad). The Quran speaks of the final battle in Dabiq that will be fought by "an army from the east wearing long beards bearing the names of their homeland."

Several people in the field of counterterrorism studies have speculated as to why bin Laden chose not to change his name. Some say, his father's name was more important to him than any ideological metamorphosis. Others have said that things moved too quickly for him, and the world came to know him by his real name too soon. Some even say, as one of (15–27, no one knows for sure) siblings by his father, keeping his father's name was in some way maintaining a connection, albeit a tenuous one, to his father.

Another theory, embraced by the authors of this text, however, is that bin Laden never saw himself as a terrorist (it can be argued that few if any terrorists see themselves as such and would never describe their actions as those of a terrorist). We will explore this notion as we move further into the study of the founder of "The Base," (Al Qaeda). First, however, we will delve into bin Laden's religious inspiration, Wahhabism.

An Islamic extremist is not a great deal different from an extremist in any other religion. Keeping in mind, it is not our intent to provide a moral equivalency. It is our intent to offer easily understood analogies for the reader. Most devout Christians can point to a well-known individual or group within Christianity who follows a much stricter ideological vision of Christianity. Today, any older person who grew up in a Christian family can remember a time when dancing was seen as sinful and those who took part in such activity were seen as "doomed to everlasting Hell." One of the authors of this book remembers hearing stories about their father who grew up in one such Christian household where attending school dances was not permitted, nor was trick-or-treating on Halloween, as this was seen as a "pagan" holiday.

Strict interpretations of any religion can easily be seen as forms of "extremism." The principal difference between Islamic extremism and extremism in other religions is that far too many extremist groups in Islam are willing to use violence to enforce their positions.

This is a key point for the student of International Terrorism: far too many extremist groups in Islam are willing to use violence. This is not to say that other extremist groups do not resort to violence as well. We know that they do and we know that there are growing threats from many extremist groups today, including white supremacist groups. Considering Islamist groups, however, there was a point in Islam when this extremist viewpoint was well-developed and verbalized and, to an extent, codified within the culture, and that point had its beginnings with Muhammad ibn Abd Wahhab, the Sunni founder of Wahhabism (the ideology embraced by the men like Osama bin Laden and most other terrorist leaders).

As stated earlier in this text, Wahhab was a reformist leader. In Islam as is the case in most religions, reformers always arise in times of trouble and always preach a return to basics, in this case the basic promise of Allah, that Muslims would always prosper if they followed his word and would always fail if they strayed from it.

The problem with this, however, is that it always involves a "sweeping away" of things that have become traditional and seemingly sacred, and it is always based upon the most prominent voice's interpretation of Allah's words and instructions (in far too many of these cases, "prominent" simply means loudest). In Islam, these words come from the Quran (Quran) and the Hadith. The Hadith is a collection of comments and sayings that came from The Prophet Mohammad and some of his closest friends and associates, rather than Allah. The Hadith is often consulted for a quick revelation or answer to a perplexing question or situation (sort of an Islamic version of "what would Jesus do," in this case, "what would Muhammad do").

Abdul Wahhab was not an instant success in his endeavors and his campaign to reinvent Islam in his view. As a matter of fact, many people at the time thought he was crazy. He had a reputation in many circles synonymous with the modern day man on the street with the clapboard sign hanging around his neck broadly proclaiming, "The End is Near." He had three things going for him however: he had a small but growing following who were more than willing to "lop off the heads" of anyone who did not embrace his ideology; he was revealing his version of Mohammad's message at a time when the actual message was still relatively unclear to recent converts, so the simple fact was folks didn't know for sure whether he was right, therefore giving him the benefit of the doubt (which was not difficult with a sword hanging over your bent over neck); and finally he had a fairly prominent figure, Mohammad ibn Saud, the founder of the Saudi royal family, among his followers and supporters. Of course, it is highly probable that Saud himself had tied his fortunes to those of Wahhab more for a form of "political gain" than as a result of a committed religious awakening, but the end result was the same; Wahhab's movement grew stronger and faster, and soon, Wahhabism was born and is still extremely influential today with 70% of the population embracing this extremist form of Islam, one of its most prominent followers being the late Osama bin Laden.

Abdul Wahhab split with the traditional mainstream Islamic community around the mid-1700s and began preaching his extremist viewpoints, building a sizable following. As stated, he formed an alliance with Mohammad Saud, the man most people see as the founding father of the Saudi royal family. Again, there is at least a strong likelihood that ibn Saud didn't necessarily embrace Wahhabism for ideological reasons, rather that, as he was politically minded, even at this time (even though rule by the Saudi family isn't dependent on a democratic vote, all leaders who choose to remain in power for a long period of time knew and still know that they need/needed the support of the majority of people over whom they reign, and Islamic leaders were routinely being bumped off in this time), he saw Wahhab had a large following.[1] Aziz ibn-Saud may have been in total agreement with Wahhab's brand of Islam, but he was also pragmatic. He later married one of Wahhab's daughters, a practice at that time used as much to seal a familial and/or political relationship, as to gain a marriage partner.

A reasonably well-supported argument can be made that Abdul Wahhab, using the vehicle of the (by this time) established Islamic religion Wahhabism, paved the way for the most egregious violence against other Muslims, particularly Shiite Muslims, though the early Wahhabists did not shy away from killing Sunni Muslims who would not embrace their form of extremist Islam. As example, in the year 1800, a horde of Wahhabist warriors led by Abdul himself rose up out of the desert on the outskirts of the principally Shiite-occupied holy city of Karbala, the site of the slaughter of Imam Hussain and his people in 680 AD. They stormed the city, the holiest site in Shiite Islam, killing thousands in the most brutal manner. Their penchant was to slice open the bellies of pregnant women pulling their unborn from the womb and displaying them on a stick above the bodies of the dead mothers[2] (a practice that was repeated in later years as descendants of the Saud family carried out similar slaughters of Shiite).

Less than a year later, they converged on the city of Medina and began systematically destroying all the tombs and grave sites, including that of the Prophet Mohammad, because they were elaborately marked and decorated and such is abhorred by the Wahhabists. Their dogmatic beliefs and practices were simple and brutally enforced, and it is safe to say that the early Wahhabists definitely defined and sanctioned torture and brutality as a way to "spread the word."

A curious dichotomy played out however in the relationship between al-Zarqawi, the founder of present-day ISIS, and Osama bin Laden, to whom Zarqawi initially pledged his allegiance. Bin Laden was an early convert to Wahhabism and remained a devout Wahhabist until his death at the hands of US Navy SEALS in 2011. Zarqawi probably was a Wahhabist, but he never overtly proclaimed such. In this light however, Zarqawi was much more overtly brutal than bin Laden, and bin Laden often chastised him for wantonly killing other Muslims. Bin Laden himself never made a practice of killing fellow Muslims whether Sunni or Shiite, preferring to win their support through other means. Bin Laden could never have been accused of being an "Abdul Wahhab-styled" Wahhabist. Many analysts have speculated as to whether bin Laden would have been more brutal in his tactics in the years following 9/11 if Zarqawi had never emerged on the scene. Still others have speculated that bin Laden, who was never directly involved in the planning for 9/11 (though it is clear he gave the go-ahead and paid for it, and knew full well it would occur), was not prepared for the carnage that resulted. This is in no way an attempt to absolve him in any manner. It is clear that it never would have happened had it not been for bin laden, but some opine that he was ill-prepared for the result.

As for Wahhab, again, one of his principal objections was to the traditional veneration and recognition of the tombs of the saints. He felt that such recognition was akin to idolatry. As a side note that we will explore further in the text, during the Russian invasion and war in Afghanistan, when the Saudi Arab fighters went to fight alongside the primarily "Pashtun," Afghan Mujahideen, they often demanded that the Afghans tear down the grave markers in the Afghan cemeteries, a demand that more than once led to serious conflicts between these allies in war (note: the typical Mujahideen fighter was illiterate and from a poor existence, and often saw bin Laden's Saudi fighters as elitists and ostentatious).[3]

Abdul Wahhab even orchestrated the destruction of the tomb of Zayd ibn al-Khattab, a companion of Mohammad, again, because within his extremist ideology, it was an affront and represented idolatry. That said, Wahhabism developed into one of the long-lasting and most influential forms of Islamic doctrine. It is the strictest form of Islamic worship and endorses the harshest standards of treatment of those who stray from its teachings. For purposes of this study, the student can easily view Wahhabism, on the one hand, and the more liberal forms of Islam, embracing aspects of westernization, on the other, as polar opposites with absolutely no prospects of "meeting in the middle, or compromise." "In a nutshell," this serious theological disagreement epitomizes the relationship between Osama bin Laden and the Saudi royal family, as well as the relationship between Ayman al-Zawahiri and the Egyptian government, as well as the relationship between Abu Musab al-Zarqawi and the government of Jordan.[1] These twisted, resentment-filled differences provided the principal impetus for, and fueled, the terroristic futures embraced by these three terror leaders and most of the men who followed and still follow them.

OSAMA BIN LADEN'S EMBRACE OF WAHHABISM

One thing that is always prevalent in Islamic terrorist operations and activities is the foundation of a strict "Quranically" substantiated stamp of approval by the highest ranking religious leader available, for all actions. For this reason, terrorist leaders always have their chosen religious leader close at hand. When, for instance (as did Musab Zarqawi), you are going to order a suicide bomb attack on an Islamic wedding celebration in which you know hundreds of women and children will be killed, it is vital that a learned religious leader put a stamp of approval on such an action, designating it as Quranically-supported and within God's will (a Zarqawi follower at that time would say, "its Gods will that these people give up their earthly life. They are today, in Heaven with Allah").

There are volumes of research on Osama bin Laden, so we will not recreate these here, in this text. We will, however, present related anecdotal topics we hope will be of interest to the reader and give some context that may be valuable in understanding the man and events that led him to his end, and again, in following the theme of this text, we will do so in a manner that hopefully helps the reader/student form some understanding of the motives and actions, based on shared human emotions.

> *Author's note: We've said this before and may repeat the assertion, but we are in no way attempting to excuse these actions; we are simply trying to engender some basic understanding. Remember, in order to defeat or control an adversary or enemy, it is vital to understand them as much as possible.*

In doing so, we will occasionally reference some long-understood aspects of bin Laden's life and family structure, but only to provide context to the anecdotes. We will additionally point out his crossing of paths with other terrorists and would-be terrorists and how these relationships influenced the actions of all involved.

> *Author's Note: In relation to your timeline, we recommend creating a line connoting bin Laden's progression and reference all others to his, since he is probably the most well-known terror leader of this generation.*

To begin with (this applies to all the terror group leaders we will discuss in this text, not just bin Laden), in order to understand to the extent possible the how's and why's of this study into individuals, you have to understand and accept the fact that they are all human beings and, from an emotional standpoint, not a lot different from you or I. You don't have to try to form any moral equivalency to the things they've done, and as a matter of fact, we have no qualms in asserting that the things they've done, to a great extent, separate them from normal humankind in terms of the brutality and inhumane results of their actions.

This text however is not written as an attempt to judge, it is intended as a tool to help the student of International Terrorism and Counterterrorism develop some understanding of the motivations and the driving factors. We can't fight against something we do not understand. If one can understand, one can defeat or at least mitigate much more successfully.

In this vein, remember that most if not all these individuals were/are sane: not good, not evil, not justified in any way, just sane. And as sane individuals, they aren't a great deal different from me or you in terms of their emotional responses to similar stimuli. In other words, they experience the same emotions, to a greater and lesser degree, granted, but the same emotions you and I experience, based on similar events and stimuli.

If you accept and apply this fact, you may be able to understand a bit more as to the "why's and the how's." In this sense, it is often helpful to try and put yourself in their place and ask yourself, "what would I be feeling, or experiencing in similar circumstances, and how would I react?" This may be a very uncomfortable exercise, but vitally important for an impartial analysis, nonetheless. Now, modify the reaction to fit more closely to bin Laden, Zarqawi, Azam or whomever, and you're a step closer to a clearer understanding.

In relation to bin Laden's embracing of Wahhabism, it is safe to say that virtually all terror leaders had a "historic hero" they emulated and followed to a great extent in their actions.[4] Bin Laden's hero happened to be Abdul Wahhab and the ideology he founded, Wahhabism. Today, roughly 65 to 70% of Saudis identify as Wahhabists, though they prefer the term "muwahidoon (believers in the one God).

Once again, the father of the Saudi royal family, Abdul Aziz ibn-Saud likely as much for political as religious reasons, embraced Wahhab and Wahhabism; therefore for the kingdom of Saudi Arabia (remember at this time Saudi Arabia had not discovered oil and was not the economic power it is today), Wahhabism was the preeminent religious doctrine. This worked fine until Saudis got rich. Wealth tends to open the eyes of even the most religiously vigorous to possibilities that may exist, and things and experiences which may be purchased, outside the strict control of a doctrine such as Wahhabism. Therefore, today, in Saudi Arabia, we see a sort of dichotomy, in which the Mutawa (religious police) may spend the day publicly chastising women for being unveiled in public and then drive home in a western-designed luxury vehicle past billboards depicting women in various forms of lesser covering and men playing musical instruments, a pastime strictly prohibited by Wahhabism.

This is the dichotomy in which Osama bin Laden grew up. A highly similar dichotomy faced the aforementioned Zawahiri and Zarqawi, as well as religious leader Sayyid Qutb and Abdullah Azam, bin Laden's associate and founder of Hamas and co-founder of Al Qaeda. This dichotomy fueled all their efforts at resistance and their eventual embrace of terrorism.

For bin Laden, the straw that broke the ubiquitous "back of the camel" was when his country embraced a relationship with the United States in its fight against Saddam Hussain's invasion of Kuwait in 1991. Bin Laden met with the King of Saudi Arabia when he learned that this would happen and requested that he (bin Laden) be allowed to lead his army (the army he had developed to help the Afghans defeat the Russians in Afghanistan) against Hussain assuring the Saudi King that an alliance with the west would not be necessary. He assured the King that his army was successful in Afghanistan and was adequate to defend the Kuwaitis without America's help. Remember, if a non-Muslim sets foot on Islamic soil, for the extremist such as Wahhabists, it is an extreme insult to them personally and to Islam as a whole. The magnitude of this insult is difficult to imagine, when considering the infraction committed by an entire non-Muslim army.

The King pretty much laughed him off, much like an adult would smile dismissively at a child's immature hubris. Recalling our instruction to compare your typical emotional responses to a stimulus, this would be a good time to try and determine how bin Laden must have felt. Also, keep in mind that within the Middle Eastern culture, humiliation is an emotion that is not easily overcome. Humiliation, once bestowed upon a person of Middle Eastern descent, can hound that person their entire life and often transcend upon their family as well.

The concepts of honor and humiliation for a westerner do not begin to equate to Middle Eastern religiously-based cultural values. Honor is everything to them. Bringing honor to oneself and one's family is of utmost importance. Humiliation of one can cause an entire family or even clan to become humiliated.

There are many documented instances where women have been killed in gruesome ways (stoning, lit on fire, beheading, acid thrown on them) when they have brought dishonor upon themselves or their family, and such continues today in many parts of the world. As the authors composed this book, a check in the daily news headlines highlighted a story from Iran in which a young couple was arrested. This couple was unmarried, and yet associated together. These two individuals were athletes that enjoyed the exhilarating extreme sport of parkour which is described as "moving from point 'a' to point 'b' using the obstacles in your path to increase your efficiency."[5]

After completing a parkour session, they were photographed on a rooftop, kissing and caressing. This physical touch between two unmarried individuals was enough to imprison them both. It can be assumed with some degree of confidence that the young woman has now brought shame and dishonor to her entire family, not to mention herself due to these "vulgar acts" (Figure 5.1).[6]

This would also be a good time to update your timeline in terms of bin Laden's development, noting his entreaty to the Saudi King.

Osama bin Laden was born in 1957 to a wealthy family in Saudi Arabia. This is important because it is illustrative to have an understanding of the status of his father and his entire family in terms of the relationship to the royal family. The bin Ladens in Saudi would be synonymous to the Kennedys in America (Kennedys and Vanderbilts are among families who are considered by most to be the closest thing the United States has had to royal families), though they had no established political positions.

Bin Laden was the 17th of 54 children in the family (the portion of a Saudi's name, "bin" usually lower case and sometimes spelled "ibn" depending on where it is in the name structure, means "son of"). His mother, one of 22 wives, was Syrian (bin Laden's father never had more than four wives at any one time, divorcing older ones and marrying younger ones in order to keep the total number at "four" since that is the prescribed maximum number of wives a man should have according to the Quran). Osama's mother was divorced shortly after she gave birth to him, so his father could take on a younger wife.[7]

This presents your first opportunity to muse, "how would I feel?" Though one of the authors of this text has a PhD in Psychology, we will not attempt to any real extent to "psychoanalyze" the man; however, the family structure, though not uncommon in wealthy Saudi families, must have generated some developing personality quirks, or possibly strengths, depending on your perspective. Osama bin Laden's father died in a plane crash in 1967 when bin Laden was ten years old. Growing up without a father has a great effect on a person's psyche and, to some extent, contributes to the paths that one decides to take in life.

In such a Saudi family, it is traditional for the oldest son (oldest male sibling) of any one particular mother to sort of take on the role of the father to some extent, to the other children from his mother (his own full blood brothers and sisters). Bin Laden, being the oldest in this sense,

Figure 5.1 Screen capture of the couples' posted video, and the image resulting in severe punishment by the state.

would have assumed this role. This is additionally important from a psychological standpoint since he would not have had an older brother to turn to at appropriate times. This may or may not have had an effect on the decisions he made later in life, but certainly had a role in shaping the person that bin Laden would become.

Here again, we should pause and note that bin Laden, exposed to the same familial background and structure as all his other 54 siblings, was the only one to have embraced such a track in life. It is safe to say that there was/were impacting events in his early life that encouraged him to embrace such profound ideologies and life choices since he grew to be so different from his siblings.

It is worth considering, for instance, that bin Laden's father was very much like all those within the very structure bin Laden grew to hate. He (the father) was very close to the royal family, he was rich and evidence indicates he didn't really shy away from the benefits and positive effects of being rich. There's no indication that he turned his back on the things enjoyed by those west-embracing moderates in Saudi society, as bin Laden did in later life, and there is absolutely no indication that the father was opposed to the King's embrace of western assistance that, for instance, would eventually allow him to call on America for assistance. Of course, the father was dead by the time bin Laden had drawn the ire of the Saudi royal family and had eventually lost his citizenship and been asked to leave Saudi Arabia, but it would have been interesting to see how the father would have reacted to the direction in life, taken by his son, and to the son's vehement opposition to the King.

Of note here is the fact that bin Laden's mother and father divorced soon after his birth and the mother remarried, so this may all be insignificant. We know that in his adult life, bin Laden took great pride in living a pious life devoid of luxuries. The authors wonder if it's possible that bin Laden shied away from all riches and associations with the royal family in an attempt to be nothing like his father? Perhaps he held resentment for his father leaving, never being there for him, and didn't want to be anything like him. We don't know this to be fact, but it is an interesting point to ponder when analyzing his character and behavior throughout his life.

Bin Laden was said to have been very close to his mother, but as you may expect, especially in light of the divorce when he was young, in a family with 1 father and 54 children, he probably had little to do with his father. The bin Laden family patriarch did provide generously for his children, sending them all to the finest schools they wanted to attend (the bin Laden family was the wealthiest family in Saudi next to the Saudi royals).

Though many of the bin Laden children went abroad to study, Osama graduated from King Abdul Aziz University in 1979 with a degree in economics.[8] It was there he met two people who would be prominent in his jihadi life, Abdullah Azam and Ayman al-Zawahiri.

Azam was a fiery, jihadist-style lecturer who preached revolution and jihad against any government that would embrace western ideals and thus distance itself from pure Islam. Bin Laden and Zawahiri were both students of Azam. Azam and Zawahiri would later join and help bin Laden form and nurture Al Qaeda during the Soviet occupation of Afghanistan, and of course, at the writing of this text, Ayman al-Zawahiri is still the ipso facto leader of Al Qaeda.[8] Bin Laden went to Afghanistan almost immediately after graduating, to assist the Afghan resistance in its fight against the Russians (for purposes of the timeline, you should document each time bin Laden returned to Saudi, then left again since he would finally leave for good, and this particular departure from his homeland should be precisely documented on timeline).

NOTES

1 Wright, L. (2006). *The terror years: From Al Qaeda to the Islamic State.* Knopf Publishing.
2 Trofimov, Y. (2008). *The siege of Mecca: The forgotten uprising in Islam's holiest shrine and the birth of al-Qaeda.* Anchor Publishing.
3 Rashid, A. (2010). *Taliban.* Yale University Press.
4 McCants, W. (2015). *The ISIS apocalypse: The history, strategy, and doomsday vision of the Islamic State.* St Martins Publishing.
5 WFPF. (n.d.). What is parkour? https://wfpf.com/parkour/.
6 Oppenheim, M. (2020, May 23). Parkour athletes arrested after image of kiss atop Tehran skyline shared online. *Independent.* https://www.independent.co.uk/news/world/middle-east/iran-parkour-kissing-alireza-japalaghy-pho to-arrest-a9529961.html.
7 Hamida al-Attas. (n.d.). In *Wikipedia.* Retrieved May 22, 2020, from https://en.wikipedia.org/wiki/Hamida_al-Attas.
8 Coll, S. (2018). *Directorate S: The C.I.A. and America's secret wars in Afghanistan and Pakistan.* Penguin Press.

6

What about Russia?

RUSSIA'S ROLE IN THE RISE OF TERRORISM AND TERRORIST ORGANIZATIONS: BEGINNING WITH OSAMA BIN LADEN

The Russian invasion, much like the invasions of every other country throughout history that had invaded Afghanistan, left its mark on that country.[1] The most immediate and impacting mark left by Russia was a nation that was more heavily mined than any other in the world. There may have been some intent in this (albeit never proven or even asserted, for that matter), but Russia left enough arms for every man, woman and child in the country to have at least two or three AK47 assault rifles as well as a few shoulder-fired rockets with launchers, just for good measure. Analogous to leaving the door to an unending supply of all manner of alcohol, open for a bunch of alcoholics, militia groups all over the country immediately began stockpiling and caching tons and tons of weapons, including fully functional Russian MIG jets fighters (one of the authors of this text personally took part in recovery of a cache belonging to Rashid Dostum in the northwest city of Maymana that took three weeks, and additional recovery of a fully operational MIG jet that had been buried by Dostum's militia members for later use). As late as 2003 in the northern city of Mazer e Shariff, for instance, almost every ten-year-old playing in the streets had an AK47 slung over his shoulder as if it were an afterthought (Figure 6.1).

Armed in such a manner, following the retreat of Russia from Afghanistan, many of the Mujahideen "holy warriors" battling the Russians morphed into Al Qaeda, the Taliban and even ISIS, transferring

(a)

(b)

Figure 6.1 Images of Northern Alliance weapons cache of weapons left by the Russians.
(Source: Author's personal photos).

their hatred for, and fight against Russia, to a hatred for and a fight against America and the west. Most of these fighters were obviously Afghans and the majority joined the Taliban (the Taliban is a regional group to date found only in Afghanistan, though many analysts have predicted they may carry their brand of terrorism to the international stage, as have Al Qaeda and ISIS), but many of them had come from Saudi at the behest of bin Laden.

It is important here to understand the world situation when the Afghan Mujahideen (holy warriors) were fighting against the Russians, because many of these same mujahideen would later become the Taliban and would later, as stated, make up the majority of terror groups around the Middle East.[2] As mujahideen (often referred to by American forces as "muj") fighters, they were heroes. As the terrorists, they were and still are enemies of the free world. Of course, only a few of the "Russian battling" brave mujahideen fighters from Afghanistan became Taliban. Many others became sworn enemies of the Taliban, most of them making up the famed Northern Alliance fighters. Some, of course, just "went home," though there was little left of "home."[3]

These young men, having fought in a decades-long war, in the most primitive conditions for the times, found themselves in much the same position our American servicemen found themselves in, following the Vietnam war. They were warriors first; normal young men, second. Joining and fighting with groups like the Taliban and Al Qaeda just seemed natural. Bin Laden went through a similar metamorphosis, albeit on a much different scale.

As for the Russians, they, like most invaders or crusaders who attempt the takeover of an entire nation, did so initially with good intentions ("good," from their perspective). They had moved slowly into the Kabul area and began to establish communism as a predominant philosophy, or governing ideology, long before the full Russian invasion and total occupation. In doing so, they were emboldened initially because the people more or less welcomed the prosperity, jobs, education for women and general improvements to their way of life, in Kabul. The Russians however were shortsighted.[4]

The Russians made the same mistake other erstwhile occupiers of this nation have; they ignored the fact that, due to the extreme rural existence of Afghans, what "flies" in Kabul doesn't necessarily work anywhere else in the country. This is a key point to take note of and one of which the Russians were unaware.

71

The Russians soon became the bad guys, and virtually, the whole world saw them as such (remember Vietnam was still fresh in the minds of Americans and the Russians, in that conflict, had been instrumental in the humiliating defeat and withdrawal of American forces from that country). Conversely, at least to America, anyone who fought the Russians was the good guy.

Muslims the world over were crawling all over each other to answer the call to jihad in defense of Islam and heading off to Afghanistan. These were heady days in the Middle East, and the mujahideen were analogous to the French Resistance (David, fighting an immense "Goliath") fighting against the Germans during WWII. Many long-lasting terrorist's relationships were begun and sealed in that place, in those days.

For the Muslim warrior (mujahideen), it must have been a happy, exciting time even though the war itself was brutal. Until funding started filtering through to them, many fought in the mountains with single shot, British Enfield rifles or something more primitive, and many wore rags on their feet in the brutal cold of the Hindu Kush mountains, and all the while, the world cheered them on[5]. This fueled them emotionally.

Though most nations, including America, supported the mujahideen, few were willing to openly fund them for fear of generating an official conflict with Russia. A young Osama bin Laden, however, was under no such restriction, and fate had decreed that he had the wealth and resources comparable to a small nation to play with.

So, to set the stage, you have a young, uber-rich, Osama bin Laden, who happens to be a devout Wahhabist, answering the call to a battle within which even his future enemies wish him well and cheer him on. Bin Laden, in addition to being rich, was also fairly politically astute. Possibilities of the situation were not lost on him.

Bin Laden probably didn't know for sure what he was going to do to help when he first went to Afghanistan, but he wasn't a "warrior" in any strict sense. In actuality, though bin Laden was a terrorist and, few would argue, earned his ultimate title, he wasn't possessed of the hate and extreme anger that drove others like Zarqawi or Azam, or the former leader of ISIS, Abu Bakr al-Baghdadi. As a matter of fact, he didn't even "hate" the Shiite to the extent these other Sunni leaders did. Bin Laden's mother, as a matter of fact, grew up in Syria in a family of Alawites, a branch of Shia Islam.[6] Bin Laden, many would argue, dreamed of a unified Islam where Sunni and Shiite joined together to form the Caliphate that would reemerge and rule the world.

Of course most of the people who went to fight weren't traditional warriors, they were just "mad as hell." Bin Laden, Zarqawi and Azam knew how to manipulate and put to use this hatred. Bin Laden himself however had a very important weapon and intended to use any and all of it if necessary, his money.

As soon as he graduated, bin Laden traveled to Peshawar, in Pakistan's Northwest Frontier Province. The area was only 15 miles or so from the border with Afghanistan, and as neutral territory, it was a perfect place to set up operations. There, he joined his old teacher Abdullah Azam who had gone there to assist with the wounded from the fighting across the border. Azam had established an organization, Maktab al-Khidamat (Services Bureau), into which bin Laden began funneling money. The money provided by bin Laden was used to fund individuals coming to the country to fight, as well as establish and fund training areas. The organization and operation later became known as "The Base" (Al Qaeda).

It is important to take a moment here and give a cursory examination to the role Pakistan played during this time. It is also important to understand what they did, why they did it and what their concerns were. Pakistan had two major concerns at the time. First, they did not want to make an enemy of Russia. As such, they never entered the war on either side. If they had however, it is doubtful it would have been, for political purposes, on the side of Russia. Pakistan was a country primarily ruled by the higher ranking members of the military, and they were as much Islamist fundamentalists as they were moderates.[7] These individuals all supported the mujahideen; however, they weren't the principal decision-makers, and even if they had been, they would have been forced to openly side with Russia. Pakistan, in consideration for long-term strategy, didn't particularly want a secular country on their border and definitely not a major super power, "secular country," and definitely-definitely not a secular, major super power that held a grudge against them for assisting their opponent in the war; therefore, whatever they did had to be done through proxies or very discreetly.

The second major concern Pakistan had, they still have, is that, to their east, they shared a border with another country they'd been warring on and off with, for generations, India. The fighting between Pakistan and India had since 1947 centered primarily on a disputed area called Kashmir. A rebellion against India, fought by Kashmiri rebels and supported by Pakistan, had at that time and has to date been ongoing. The area is populated predominantly by Muslims who want independence from predominantly Hindu, India. In comes Osama bin Laden.

Bin Laden's primary objective was to assist the mujahideen in their struggle against Russia. In doing so, he set up training camps just inside Afghanistan near a place called Tora Bora. If you were to examine a map of the western border of Pakistan, the border with Afghanistan, in the center of the border, you'd see something that resembles a man's profile with a prominent nose extending into Afghanistan. Tora Bora is along the top side of the "nose" landmass protruding into Afghanistan (Figure 6.2).

Just east further inland in Pakistan is Peshawar, where bin Laden was headquartered. This area (Tora Bora) is important for several reasons, as bin Laden was bringing top-line Arab fighters into Pakistan and sending them to Tora Bora to train Afghan mujahideen fighters. Pakistan was supportive of this in addition to all the aforementioned reasons, because bin Laden was also funding the training of Pakistani rebels to go to Kashmir and fight alongside the Kashmiri rebels.

The area is also important because this is the last place America came into contact with bin Laden before he and his top commanders disappeared into Pakistan.[7]

It is noteworthy that though bin Laden never actually took part in much of the actual fighting in Afghanistan, preferring to be more of a financier and "backseat driver," he did take part in one major battle against the Russians, and it too was in this immediate area. Those famous photos of bin Laden walking down a mountainside using a cane were taken in this area as well.

Author's Note: The pictures released at the time were taken in the vicinity of Tora Bora where Osama bin Laden was operating primarily, and from where he made his final escape into Pakistan while American troops were attempting to apprehend him and his commanders. The area was narrowed down and ultimately identified, from this picture through the assistance of geologist Dr. John, "Jack" Shroder of University of Nebraska at Omaha. Dr. Shroder first visited Afghanistan in 1973 as the head of Kabul University seismic station. When he saw the Al Jazeera videotape from which the two pictures were taken, he recognized the formations behind bin Laden. Working with the US government, he was able to narrow the location to an approximate 20 square mile area to allow the FBI to more closely pinpoint bin

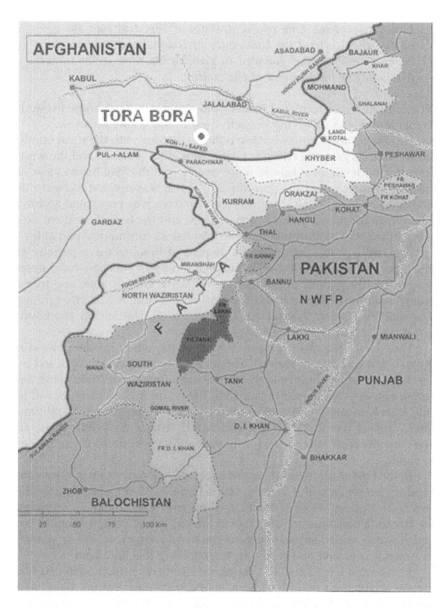

Figure 6.2 Tora Bora area in Eastern Afghanistan.
(Source: Image retrieved and used from Wikipedia, per Creative Commons 3.0.
Created and posted by user Victor Falk, 2007).

Laden's location. One of the authors of this text had the opportunity to attend the University of Nebraska's "Afghanistan Immersion Program" founded in part by Dr. Shroder and hear firsthand the background of this action.[8]

When the Russians retreated in 1989, bin Laden returned home to Saudi Arabia and began involving himself more in the family business.

He also began a slowly boiling political dispute with the royal family mostly over its growing friendly relationship with America and the west. To better understand this, you must realize that the Wahhabist view of the west, America and the non-Muslim world, was not just a slight difference of opinion. Their view was that America was populated and led by enemies of Islam, apostates and infidels, and the hatred for them was and still today is within much of the Wahhabist community palpable.

It is difficult to understand the depths of this feeling, especially at this time, but gaining a bit of an understanding of such provides great insight into the actions of bin Laden, Al Qaeda, Islamic State and terror groups operating today around the world. That said, it was through this lens that bin Laden viewed America and any relationship the Saudi Royal family had with America.

The "coup de grâce" appeared a year later, when Saddam Hussain ordered the invasion of Kuwait. The invasion was of course opposed by almost every other country in the world, including Saudi Arabia (and bin Laden himself, as a matter of fact), and the world immediately moved to side with Kuwait. America of course backed its opposition with military force, and as the Royal family and Saudi Arabia were our allies, an agreement was struck to launch American military opposition from bases in Saudi.

In the best of times, fundamentalist Saudi Arabian Muslims view non-Muslims presence in the country that is home to Mecca and Medina, the two holiest places in all of Islam, as abhorrent. Even today, it is against the law for a non-Muslim to set foot in Mecca.[9] As one might imagine, bin Laden was horrified at the thought of not just an American, but thousands of Americans armed and ready for war, defiling this holy land.

He went to King Fahd and expressed his dismay (bin Laden had this type of access because of his family connections and wealth). Bin Laden tried to convince the King that he still had the army he had trained and funded to defeat the Russians in Afghanistan, and they were more than adequate to defeat the army of Saddam Hussain and kick him out of Kuwait. As stated earlier in this text, reports are that the King and his advisors responded in much the way an adult would to an errant, though, ambitious child, and the offer was summarily dismissed, as was bin Laden. The result was an intensified hatred on the part of Osama bin Laden for the royal family and a magnified hatred for America.

Shortly afterward, bin Laden began to issue only slightly veiled threats against the royal family and America and made his feelings known to his followers and to the thousands of fundamentalists and Wahhabists in Saudi Arabia. Soon, and to a degree at the behest of America, Saudi stripped him of his citizenship, and he along with his family fled to Afghanistan (keep in mind that during this time, bin Laden fled several locations always with his extended family, and always in luxury, in a couple of modified Ariana jets, and most often as a result of pressure on those countries from America, which of course only intensified his hatred for the United States).

Afghanistan in the best of situations didn't offer the comfort and luxury that bin Laden was used to so he moved again, that same year (1991), to Khartoum, Sudan. By 1999, Afghanistan and the area around Khartoum, Sudan, had both become the perfect "Hole in the Wall" (a reference to bandit hideouts in the wild west in the 1800s) for many of the world's committed terrorists. Bin Laden took advantage of both locations at various times, eventually settling back in Afghanistan in 1996.

"HOLE IN THE WALL" FOR INTERNATIONAL TERRORISTS

In the American west, there was a location in the Wyoming Mountains referred to as "Hole in the Wall." Its infamy was a result of the fact that many of the region's outlaws and wanted cattle rustlers used it from time to time as a retreat, where they could rest and recuperate before launching their next venture into lawlessness. Visitors to the area during the time included Billy the Kid, Jesse James, and Butch Cassidy and the Sundance Kid. Of course, stories about Hole in the Wall down through the ages have been greatly exaggerated, as have the movies and books referencing the area, but the basics relevant to its existence and use are fairly accurate.

Khartoum, Sudan, held a similar reputation primarily due to its sharing a border with Egypt, Libya and several relatively destitute African nations including Ethiopia. Its reputation, deserved or not, was amplified in the early 1990s when Osama bin Laden settled there, opening a terrorist training camp (one among many opened in Sudan by several other nations and terror groups) and launching a couple of legitimate businesses. Sudan made it to America's list of countries sponsoring terrorism in 1993 and gained a similar recognition from the United Nations in 1996.

RETIRED SPECIAL FORCES SERGEANT MAJOR BILLY WAUGH, NOT THE FRENCH

Early one morning in the spring of 1994, retired Special Forces SGM (Sergeant Major) Billy Waugh, now contracted to the CIA's paramilitary wing as an operations officer, was sitting in his favorite coffee shop relaxing before his day's routine kicked in. He had been sent to Khartoum to surveil Osama bin Laden, a man of interest to the world's intelligence community, and about whom relatively little was known (https://www.google.com/search).

Suddenly, through the door in walked a middle aged African male who from his physique was obviously a very adept and practiced bodybuilder. Such an occurrence would have raised few eyebrows if it hadn't been for the fact that bodybuilders were as rare as unicorns in Khartoum, Sudan. Additionally, SGM Waugh was a highly experienced, savvy counterintelligence operative and observant of everyone he encountered in Africa's very own "Hole in the Wall." He had also read several (at the time, classified) missives about Carlos the Jackal (Ilich Ramirez Sanchez), who was still on the run and highly elusive, and knew that, although there were very few pictures of the man himself, he was known to be constantly in the company of a beautiful women and a close friend and bodyguard who happened to be a black male and accomplished bodybuilder. Not "a great leap," in intelligence terms, especially considering the location, SGM Waugh deduced that Carlos was nearby.

He followed the bodybuilder to a local high-end hotel and determined that it was probably a good location to set up a permanent overwatch. Temporarily suspending his work on bin Laden who was an easy target for surveillance since he seemed not to be going anywhere anytime soon, SGM Waugh developed a plan with his men to set around the clock surveillance on the hotel in hopes a likely fit for "The Jackal" would emerge. At the same time, they coordinated a distraction plan to enable them to more easily secure the terrorist and his bodyguard.

The plan was simple. A local street vendor who often set up operations on the sidewalk just outside the hotel entrance and a young man, at the appropriate signal, would get into an altercation attracting the attention of the targets, while SGM Waugh and his men would move in and take them into custody.

Finally one morning, three days into the overwatch, the bodyguard stepped cautiously through the door followed by a man dressed in expensive clothes with a beautiful woman in his arms. As the signal was given, the vendor and the young man began a loud argument followed by a few punches, and Carlos the Jackal and crew were totally mesmerized. The capture came off without a hitch and the famed Carlos the Jackal was now in the custody of retired Special Forces Sergeant Major Billy Waugh and his men.

Of course, as soon as he was booked in a cell at the local police department, and the French government, which held the most recent outstanding warrants for him, was notified, they swarmed the cell, taking custody of the prisoners and announcing to the world that the French government had finally captured Carlos the Jackal. SGM Waugh and his men went quietly back to their original task of surveillance over Osama bin Laden.

THE RISE OF THE FIRST ISLAMIC STATE LEADER, MUSAB ZARQAWI

Author's Note: We will return to Osama bin Laden in this text at a point where his life intersects with the life of the terror leader we will introduce at this point. Adjust your timeline accordingly.

In prophecy, the Hadith speaks of an army that will come from Khorasan (northern Afghanistan and northeast Iran) wearing black beards, riding under a black flag (this is why many Islamic terror groups use a black flag as a symbol of their organization, ISIS included) and made up of young men who have taken the name of their homeland. It also infers that among them will be the Mahdi, or for some, the returning conqueror.

When the bin Laden's and the Zarqawi's followers of began killing in the name of a pure Islam, they also killed Muslims. As a matter of fact, today among the group of people who make up the victims of terrorist actions throughout the world, Muslims by far outnumber every other religion or ethnicity. Most of the fundamentalist Imams, Mullahs and writers never intended this. They urged a level of zealotry, but most agree they never envisioned the wholesale slaughter of Shiite by Sunni,

79

or vice versa. In hindsight, however, it is obvious that many of the religious leaders of the day, and still today, seem to take advantage of the situation however, by speaking out when it is to their advantage and remaining silent when it is also to their advantage.

Most of the hardline clerics (though a few of them did wish to see wanton slaughter) were on more of a mission to win the hearts and minds and unite the Muslim world under one banner. Osama bin Laden himself at one point decried the slaughter being carried out by Musab Zarqawi under the banner of Al Qaeda.[10] Zarqawi's one time mentor and spiritual guide, Maqdisi, even called on him at one point to "back off." The hardline clerics wanted a level of fervor, but they wanted it to extend a short way past the doors of the Mosques and no further. They didn't account for the fact that the young men they'd be preaching to especially after the Russia/Afghan war would be young men who were used to killing and torturing, especially when they saw themselves as tools of Allah.

In the 13th century, as a matter of fact, a fiery Islamist preacher, Ibn Taymiyyah of the highly fundamentalist Hanbali school of Islam, preached among other things that there was precedent for Muslims to rise up against their Muslim leaders who had gone astray. The young men who were listening to those who would follow the likes of Taymiyyah took his words to heart, though many would argue that's not exactly what he meant.

Again, in truth these men who stoked the fires were playing a little bit of a selfish game, using and manipulating the young people they were exhorting and then hiding behind the veil of "Oh, that's not what we meant" when the heat became a little too intolerable. Saudi Arabia itself even played that game to an extent. The problem is that it was a game that was and still is very difficult to control.[11] Once it got out of hand, the participants could be hurt as badly as those they'd prefer this weapon be wielded against. One such pawn in this game, eventually adopting the nom de guerre, Abu Musab al-Zarqawi was a perfect example.

In Zarqa, Jordan, 1966, Ahmad al-Khalayleh was born. The only son among a group of eight siblings (a very important point in terms of the manner in which he was raised and pampered by his mother), his family was hard-working, middle class and well respected in the community. His mother doted on him as he grew up (Figure 6.3).

Khalayleh, on the other hand, grew to be anything but the "model son." In the relatively "western-oriented" country of Jordan, Khalayleh openly took advantage of every vice in which any American "bad kid" would indulge. He drank, smoked, used drugs and dealt with

Figure 6.3 Born Ahmad al-Khalayleh, he would become known as Abu Musab al-Zarqawi, founder of ISIS.[12]

prostitutes, even pimping for a period of time. He was a local neighborhood tough and, in addition to terrorizing the area, caused countless sleepless nights for his mother. By the time he was a young teen, he was already well-known to the police.[13]

It is important to remember that in the Middle East especially during the time Khalayleh was growing up, Jordan was a country run by a moderate royal family who encouraged western ideals to a point.

Alcohol consumption, night clubs, movie theaters that featured western-style movies and even dancing were permitted.

King Hussain, head of the Hashemite dynasty and ruler of Jordan when Khalayleh was growing up, died in 1999. This is important because of a slight mistake and misunderstanding that occurred upon King Hussain's death followed by the ascension to royalty of his son, King Abdullah, the current.

King of Jordan contributed to the reign of terror by the terrorist who was born Ahmad al-Khalayleh. These events will be discussed later in this section.

The Hashemites of Jordan, oldest living dynasty in that country, and rulers over Mecca for more than 700 years, embraced a moderate philosophy in Jordan. Khalayleh had no problem with this as a youngster, and as a matter of fact, like most delinquent juveniles, partook of every allowable vice at the time causing him to be well-known to the local police, who had taken him into custody many times. Obviously, as mentioned, Khalayleh's behavior contributed greatly to the angst of his mother.[14]

Khalayleh's mother searched continuously for some way to change the path of her son, whom she adored. Finally, she enrolled Khalayleh in a local fundamentalist Islamic religious organization, similar to a small madrassa. Keep in mind, this was the late 1980s, a time when the war in Afghanistan against the Russians had been going on for approximately nine years.

For Khalayleh, the change in atmosphere and the new environment worked. As a matter of fact, it worked much better than his mother had hoped. Overnight, Ahmad Khalayleh became a zealot, even cautioning his mother and sisters as to their actions moving about the community unveiled. Khalayleh became a changed young man, moving from the extreme end of the spectrum to the opposite "extreme end." His spiritual transformation had a profound effect on him causing a great deal of personal anguish over all his life of "sin." He vowed then and there to use the rest of his life to make up for his many sins against Allah.[14]

When the local Mullah issued a call for young men to travel to Afghanistan to join in the holy war against the Russians, Ahmad was the first in line. He truly saw this as an opportunity to cleanse his soul and actually went to Afghanistan in hopes of becoming *Shahid* (martyr).

A fairly well-established route for fighters from Jordan and the region, east through Iraq and Iran into Afghanistan, delivered him to the battle ground. As said, Ahmad al-Khalayleh arrived in Afghanistan, anxious to martyr himself in any way possible, but he wasn't a great deal different from most young Islamic men during that time.

Americans find this hard to understand, but among young extremist Muslims, especially among men who've been schooled in the hardline madrassas, there is a very definite direct pipeline for the *Shahid* from this earthly existence to paradise. During the Iran/Iraq war, young men were given plastic keys, by the Iraqi Mullahs (sort of military chaplains), and told to keep them in their pockets because they were their assurance of entry into Heaven (in a very real sense to them, their "key to Heaven") for those killed on the battlefield. The practice was highly successful as these young men fought with abandon, dying by the thousands. It's not clear whether Khalayleh was given any such tangible item, but he may as well have been. Years later, associates would remember him in the very few skirmishes he had an opportunity to take part, as almost intent on dying on the battlefield.[10]

Khalayleh was highly religious, though embarrassed at his lack of reading skills and his lack of knowledge of the Quran. He is said to have often wept loudly as he prayed.[15] There is no doubt from reports from those who knew him well during this time that he went to Afghanistan actually hoping never to return, to instead die on the battlefield. One of Zarqawi's close associates at this time was Hudaifa Azzam, son of bin Laden's associate, and Egyptian founder of Hamas, Abdullah Azam, though it is not clear whether Khalayleh ever met the father.

There is a possibility, however, that he may have met Osama bin Laden during this trip to Afghanistan. The few battles he took part in were in the vicinity of Khost Province in eastern Afghanistan close to the Pakistan border. Bin Laden funded and often visited a large training area there, which is used to train fighters for the jihad against the Russians as well as to send to the Kashmir area to fight in the rebellion against India. If he met bin Laden then, it was in passing and not a notable contact. Regardless of whether he met bin Laden during this period or not, he would in the coming years meet and have an extensive and dangerous relationship with him.

Some analysts have asserted that Khalayleh was always at odds with bin Laden, at times, shunning him and failing to swear allegiance to him even though he had declared himself founder and leader of Al Qaeda in Iraq. The truth however is that, initially, it was bin Laden who shunned Khalayleh, unsure of the young man's mental stability and controllability, when Khalayleh initially offered his services to Al Qaeda, in Afghanistan. Khalayleh actually waited for days to get an audience with bin Laden, finally meeting with a bin Laden commander instead.

He was without doubt beseeching the Al Qaeda leader begging to audition for the team, probably because he had never been able to achieve his goal of martyrdom during his short involvement in the Afghan/Russia war.

Although he had been known as a stubborn, self-aggrandizing delinquent, he had developed a reputation among the fellow jihadists close to him in those Afghan/Russia war days as humble and extremely religious. He shied away from the more learned, not wanting to demonstrate his lack of basic reading skills and his lack of knowledge of the Quran.[16] Again however, when it came to the few actual battles he was involved in, he is said to have fought recklessly and without fear of death. Khalayleh was analogous to a young teen in America who has experienced a Christian religious conversion and dove headlong into every detail and aspect of this new life and commitment to his adopted faith. We've all known people like this; people, usually young, who make severe life changes almost overnight and basically lose sight of anything relevant to the real world. Multiply such a conversion by a factor of ten, and you'll have an idea who and what Ahmad al-Khalayleh had become.

This "new and improved" "Ahmad" was the perfect prototype of the newly converted terrorist, easily pliable and eager to please those he saw as his mentors in Islam. Converts, of any religion, often try to prove themselves and their worth to that new-found religion and way of life. As such, they often go overboard and become extreme in their beliefs. It is very common for converts to change their life to follow a new set of religious rules "to the T" so-to speak. There is not the slightest consideration of diverging from what "the book" says is the right way to live-whatever book they now follow, be it the Quran, the Bible or other. Fellow Jihadists would say in later years that this "converted" Ahmad often cried uncontrollably when the Quran was read.

It is important to consider here that he was also experiencing a great deal of guilt for his former life and was in great fear that he would not be able to compensate enough in his new role as a staunch defender of fundamental Islam, before he was killed in battle. The tie that binds all this, however, is Ahmad al-Khalayleh's perception of his responsibility and his duties to Islam.

To the newly convicted (convicted within their religion; "saved," if you will) within all religions but especially Islam, a strange two-step process takes place; first, they have a clear unambiguous picture of what is required of them, and second, everything they hear, in their perception, reinforces their view. As such, Khalayleh knew who the enemies of Islam were, and he knew, beyond a doubt, that his function was to destroy them. To Ahmad al-Khalayleh, these enemies were myriad. He was in every sense of the phrase "a man on a mission from God." He had begun this mission in Afghanistan, but alas, that war had ended before he'd had time to purge himself of his sins.

Khalayleh did benefit from his time in Afghanistan, however. He had the opportunity to take part in a few small battles. He had an opportunity to "kill the enemies of Islam." He had an opportunity to prove to himself that he would not shirk from danger and was ready for the next steps. He had the opportunity to make connections and to prove himself to others as a leader. From his actions later in life, he very likely as well developed a taste for killing, especially when the killings were completely righteous in his view.

Islam, much like every other established religion in the world, is a "religion of peace." For the moderates and non-fundamentalists, those who do not adhere to strict forms of Wahhabism for instance, the use of violence to achieve any objective in Islam is not acceptable. Such may not have been the case in the early stages of the development of Islam when the Prophet Mohammad was alive and when violence to a certain degree was necessary for simple survival.

There was a time in every religion when violence was not only acceptable, and necessary, but sanctified by God. For the fundamentalist; the Wahhabist, and followers of today however, that hasn't changed and their interpretation of the Quran, the Hadith and the words of The Prophet not only sanctify killing, but promise the highest of rewards in Heaven for those who undertake to kill appropriately, in the name of Allah. To come as close as possible to understanding this, one must accept that this is the word of Allah, as it is read and interpreted by those who lead and those who follow in extremist Islam. Ahmad al-Khalayleh was the epitome of one who believed and followed such instructions, and grew to be a fairly adept leader within this realm. His "baptism of fire" as well as his journey began however humbly, on the field of battle in Afghanistan.[10]

Khalayleh was in Afghanistan taking part in the war against the Russians for less than three months when the Russians decided to leave. It must be understood here that these young men who had left their homes to take part in the fighting in Afghanistan were seen the world over as more or less heroes. They were the "David" standing up to the Russian "Goliath." For far too many of them, it ended all too soon. Khalayleh was one of these who hoped for the war to continue so he'd have time to distinguish and martyr himself. Remember, in these times and in this place, these men, many of whom would later become vicious terrorists, as well as the Mullahs and holy men who led them were seen as heroes and their efforts as noble and honorable. The world rooted for them and their victory over the Russians.

Most of them, like young men the world over, who took part in war, additionally, simply grew to love the life and times. Once the celebration was over, they were at somewhat of a loss. As stated, for Khalayleh, it definitely ended all too soon, and he would, in the coming days, return to Jordan never having reached his goal of *Shahid*.

It should also be clearly understood that when the Russians pulled out, they left untold amounts of weapons and munitions behind, including serviceable tanks artillery and even fully operable MIG jets. One of the authors of this text had the opportunity to see firsthand the sheer magnitude of weapons and munitions left behind (after it had been picked over, by the way), and it was mind-boggling. AKs were scattered on the grounds in many locations, like so many twigs having fallen from the trees. Crates of munitions, never opened, were available for the taking. To exacerbate things, movement of these items back across the border into Iran and further into Iraq and Jordan wasn't difficult (Figure 6.4).

Figure 6.4 Example of munitions discarded by Russians in the vicinity of Qala-i-Jangi.
(Source: Author's personal photo).

The borders were porous at best, and those involved in these nations' sovereignty simply hadn't foreseen a situation, such as that which now existed in the region. The simple combination of droves of young men, trained and accustomed to "the fight," no longer having a discernible enemy or for that matter, much of a purpose in life, heading home with as much of the spoils of war (in this case, weapons, explosives and munitions) as they could carry simply had not been contemplated. These men, including Khalayleh and many of his close friends, went home, with a barely quenched thirst to defend Islam. They took with them, however, as much of the means to do so as they could carry.

Once back in the region of Jordan, they wisely cached their spoils, and simply went home, with plans to meet often. Khalayleh went to work in a video store, though in his newly adopted religious fervor, he hated the idea of movies, especially western-style movies. He was naturally restless and often at odds with his mother and sisters, chiding them about their dress and the fact that they went about in public unveiled, as was the custom in Jordan. He was like a zealous recovering alcoholic, living in a house with drinkers.

SPIRITUAL ADVISOR SHEIKH ABU MUHAMMAD AL-MAQDISI

In Jordan, back in his hometown of Zarqa, Khalayleh came under the influence of Sheikh Abu Muhammad al-Maqdisi. He had met Maqdisi in Afghanistan, but the relationship was sealed once the two men were in a combat-free environment and had time to stoke one another's hatred for the Shiite and extreme Islamic ideals. As is the case in all such situations, men who feel passionate about their ideals seek out others who support their positions.

For Khalayleh, meeting Maqdisi was akin to Elvis Presley meeting Col Tom Parker. For Maqdisi, at the time, meeting Khalayleh was akin to Col Tom Parker meeting Elvis Presley. The two men, however, apparently had two very different visions for carrying out their shared goal of a new caliphate, and they also apparently never discussed the methodology. If they had, they may have split ways early on. Maqdisi was often taken aback by Khalayleh's penchant for viciousness, especially against other Muslims.

Maqdisi's vision was much more subdued. He envisioned an Islamic state but one in which all Muslims would build. He still hated the Shiite and blamed them for much of what was wrong with Islam, but he wasn't ready for the wholesale slaughter that Khalayleh was so very anxious to initiate. Muslims killing Muslims was as easy for men like Khalayleh to envision as it was impossible for men like Maqdisi. Khalayleh had been exposed to such a level of wanton violence, and Maqdisi, like most of the firebrand clerics of the time, had not. As we will see, Maqdisi would later in this evolution reject his protégé as would bin Laden and many others. At this early stage however, such a break in the unity was the farthest thing from either's mind.

This relationship between Maqdisi and Khalayleh was doubly important, since Maqdisi was a recognized religious scholar and had published his ideas widely. To put him in perspective, as most Islamic extremist ideals advocate killing of the infidel if he can't be converted, Maqdisi was a verbal proponent of moving directly to the "killing" part and not bothering with the conversion attempt, though he apparently hadn't thought this through. Once Khalayleh actually started doing this, Maqdisi got cold feet.

Earlier in this text we pointed out that the principal enemy of fundamentalist Islam is other Muslims. This is specifically true with Maqdisi and Khalayleh, and this point will be much more salient later in this section. The primary focus of their "other Muslims" hatred was the Shiite, but Khalayleh proved many times his willingness to kill Sunni Muslims if it would enhance his position or further the accomplishment of his objectives. He had convinced himself that those he killed or ordered killed, in the name of Allah, would surely be rewarded as martyrs in Heaven. Such a position or belief on the part of tyrants, whether they be terrorists or political dictators, relieves them from any burdensome conscience issues. This is vital to one who perceives himself on a mission from God/Allah, and Khalayleh definitely fell into this category.

However, the Shiites were the principal targets. To these two men, and much of the world's population of Sunni terror groups, the Shiites are infidels, dirty, loud and lazy, and can be blamed for every historic setback Islam has ever faced. The prejudices and hatred are deep-rooted and should be understood to an extent, in order to understand the actions of these men, in this time.[6]

Another "tie" that bound Maqdisi and Khalayleh lay in the fact that as Khalayleh saw himself as the "profoundly religious Muslim" and defender of Islam and Allah, he strove to be able to defend each and every action he took as "within the will of Allah." As example, at one point when he had taken the reins of leadership of Al Qaeda in Iraq, Khalayleh sent a husband/wife team of suicide bombers back to Amman to blow up a wedding celebration, killing hundreds.

The two would-be bombers (the woman backed out at the last moment and was later arrested) had never met before they were brought together at the last moment. As they were to pose as husband and wife and share the same accommodations while traveling and staying briefly in Amman before the attack, Khalayleh insisted upon them being legally married before they left.[13] Such "spiritual cleansing" and Godly acquiescence to even the most brutal acts was, and for the most part, still is, observed by religiously inspired terror organizations. Astounding though true, terrorists will adhere to these strict codes, as if this makes the act itself moral and ethical and tell themselves those that lost their lives at their hands were "chosen by God" or "unbelievers that deserved such a fate." Terrorist leaders will go to any lengths to recruit and obtain individuals willing to die for their cause. They will even use children, the elderly, the invalid and mentally handicapped. Al Qaeda used women with Down syndrome as suicide bombers in a 2008 attack that killed nearly 100 people.[17]

One of the authors of this text studied suicide bombings in Afghanistan in which the perpetrators drove to the locations with young children in the back seats of their bomb-laden vehicles, parked the car in the appropriate places and left the children in the back seat so as to assure no one's suspicion was aroused as they walked away, again assuring the children would be rewarded in Heaven.

In short, the relationship between Maqdisi and Khalayleh was almost tailor-made. Maqdisi, the ipso facto link to Allah, was not much of a tactician or planner and rarely if ever took part in actual fighting or violence, but he was a recognized religious scholar, and if he blessed an action, it was a green light for Khalayleh. Khalayleh, on the other hand, was a tactician, planner and extremely ruthless and brutal, a match made in "terror Heaven." The two were arrested together, and both were sentenced to 15 years in prison. Evidence suggests that the short time they actually did serve in prison allowed Maqdisi to mellow and realize that he wasn't prepared to "pay the piper," and it allowed Khalayleh the time to hone his skills as a leader and develop a reputation among his current and future followers.[10]

MUKABARAT, "THE FINGERNAIL FACTORY": A NECESSARY ENTITY

In part, as a response to a rise in terrorism in the region attributed to the return of these Afghan war veterans, many countries formed national security agencies to address these issues. Jordan's Mukabarat was one of these. Khalayleh and his friends weren't the only Jordanian members of the wave of Afghan veterans returning home with these extremist ideologies they'd honed in Afghanistan, though they would soon become among the most well-known.

The two forces, Khalayleh and crew and the Mukabarat, moved in their own way, heading toward a confrontation. The Mukabarat security forces, and Khalayleh and friends, who had formed a tightknit group intent on sending a message to the moderate Jordanian leadership to "mend your ways and return to fundamental Islam, or die" would soon become intertwined.

The group Khalayleh formed, Jund al-Sham (Syrian Division), eventually determined the best way to announce their presence and purpose. They surreptitiously retrieved their weapons and explosives, waiting for the perfect time to launch coordinated attacks on targets in Jordan, they deemed appropriate, due to their decadent themes.

One of these targets was a bookstore that sold magazines containing soft pornography or pictures of scantily clad women. Another was a movie theater that was known to show hardcore pornographic films. Unfortunately, though they had the fervor, they lacked the strategic and technical skills necessary to make such attacks successful. The team member assigned to blow up the theater, for instance, went into the building with his explosives concealed, sat on a seat and slowly placed the bomb under his chair. As he was preparing to leave, he suddenly became engrossed in the movie, sat back down and forgot about the bomb.[14] When it exploded, he was the only person injured, losing both his legs.

Author's Note: Now that's a story you don't usually hear about in a textbook on security and terrorism studies!

THE MERGING OF UNRELATED EVENTS

As is the case in most profound events in life, hindsight gives us a clear picture of how unrelated events merge to help or hinder such events.

The Mukabarat had little trouble in determining who was responsible for these attacks, and Maqdisis, Khalayleh and most of Jund al-Sham were soon arrested and imprisoned in one of Jordan's notorious prisons, set up specifically to hold the worst of the worst, which included this new era's would-be terrorists. Khalayleh, as ringleader, was sentenced to 15 years, along with Maqdisis. Unfortunately, the prison authorities used very poor judgment and allowed the entire gang to be held together in a single large unit, virtually ensuring they would bolster each other and simply become stronger in their commitment. In later years, prison officials would learn from these mistakes, seeing that such situations are fertile breeding grounds for future terrorists and terrorist actions.

While Khalayleh and his men began serving their sentences, then King of Jordan, King Hussein, became ill with cancer. When he knew he was going to die soon, he summoned one of his sons, Abdullah II, and informed him that he would ascend to the throne and succeed his father. King Hussein succumbed to the disease in 1999, and his son King Abdullah II took the throne.

As is the custom in such times of change in royalty in Jordan, following a long period of mourning for the passing King, additional weeks of celebratory events and customary activities took place. One of these customary acts was/is the pardoning of prisoners.

In fairness, and mildly stated, King Abdullah II had much on his plate. Informed of the "pardoning" tradition, he advised members of Parliament to give him a list of candidates for consideration. The list grew and grew until it became quite unmanageable. Anxious to maintain good relationships with his Parliament, and still overwhelmed with duties of the newly crowned King, King Abdullah simply signed off on the entire list, confident that it had been properly vetted by members of his staff. His confidence, as he would soon see, had been sorely misplaced.

Unbeknownst to him under the circumstances, on the list were Ahmad al-Khalayleh and his mentor Muhammad al-Maqdisi. In fairness, unless King Abdullah had personally vetted each and every individual with a member of the Mukabarat sitting next to him, he probably wouldn't have known who the men were, simply by their names. King Abdullah, before becoming King, had been a Special Forces soldier and helicopter pilot in the military, but had not been personally involved in terrorist operations as had the men of the Mukabarat. Once the order was signed and placed into effect, the doors of the prisons metaphorically swung open and among those walking through were Maqdisi and Khalayleh.[18]

A strange thing happened in the next two days, something that attested to the leadership skills and commitment of this young Khalayleh. Though he had been in this hell hole of a prison for five years, during which time he had cemented his relationship with the men of Jund al-Sham, in the next 24 hours, he went home, kissed his mother, cleaned up and borrowed a car, driving back out to the prison arriving there early in the morning and standing in line for visitation privileges.

When the door was opened that morning to allow visitors to enter, Khalayleh walked in, signed the roster and went directly to the cell where his men were held, just to tell them he had not forgotten them and to bolster their spirits. Such leadership abilities and skills would soon be used to terrorize much of the Middle East.

MUKABARAT AND KHALAYLEH, TIED AT THE HIP

In short order, King Abdullah was made aware of the grave error but as it was a solemn tradition and could not be reversed, there was little that could be done. The Mukabarat knew Khalayleh well enough to know who he was and what he was capable of. They had interrogated him many times. As is the case often, he had even developed a strange sort of adversarial relationship with one of the principal investigators and counterintelligence operatives, Habes al-Hanini, "nom de guerre," Abu Haytham. In the early days, Haytham, during interrogations sessions, often engaged in idle chit-chat with Khalayleh learning more about him personally, including the level of his commitment to Islamic extremist jihad. Haytham knew early on that Khalayleh was a serious player in the world of terrorism in the region and conveyed as much to King Abdullah.[13]

It was an unfortunate accident that Muhammad al-Maqdisi had also been released, but it made more sense that some parliamentarian would recommend him, since he was a very well-known religious scholar and writer. While it is true that Maqdisi harbored a great deal of hate for the perceived "enemies of his brand of Islam," which included virtually all Shiite Muslims, Maqdisi preferred to stay in the background and encourage, rather than actually take part in the "heavy work." Ironically, though in the early days, Maqdisi had advocated killing all Shiites rather than taking the time to try to convert or influence them, we will see that once the "real" killing began, orchestrated by Khalayleh, Maqdisi was apparently a little squeamish at the actual results and eventually broke with Khalayleh over the level of violence he was pursuing against other Muslims.

Such was not that unusual however since the most active influential religious scholars who cajoled and motivated the major terror leaders rarely ever took part in the actual acts of violence.

Five years in prison seemingly had the requisite effect on Maqdisi. His release was unfortunate, but didn't compare with that of Khalayleh. As stated, Khalayleh was back with his men within 48 hours encouraging them. Maqdisi wasn't heard from for a while after his release.

The men of the Mukabarat, following Khalayleh's release, did the only thing they could do under the circumstances; they watched him 24 hours of every day for weeks afterward, knocking on his door and demanding access in order to search the premises, at all hours of the day and night. As one may expect, Khalayleh's hatred for anything related to the government of Jordan and the royal family simply grew and seethed.

Finally, one day in 1999, he showed up at the airport with his mother with two tickets to Pakistan and two Pakistani visas.

INSPIRATION OF THE WOMEN IN KHALAYLEH'S LIFE

Much of this text is devoted to the "women" and their influence and involvement in the development of Islamic terror groups and terror leaders. It is pertinent to remember that even in a patriarchal society, where the men hold the status, power and freedom and have the final say over female relatives, within a family, mothers are nonetheless seen as vital.

Women, although expendable in terrorist groups, are also held in high regard in that they are the ones raising the next generation of fighters. They are the ones at home, influencing young men and women and shaping who they will become throughout their lives. Mothers, across cultures, are typically the glue that binds families together and are the core to healthy familial ties. Within Islam, this is no different. As a matter of fact, Pashtun men will never mention the name of their mother or older sister in public as it is seen as a sign of disrespect. Men will refer to their mother as *Bibi*, a universally understood title for mother or "older woman."

This information must be filtered through a sieve of basic knowledge of the relationship between men and women in the more fundamental sectors of Islam. As a caveat, it should also be understood that though widespread, not all Muslims adhere to such relationship guidelines and restrictions. As stated however, the fundamentalists, Wahhabists and these individuals make up the majority of the Islamic terrorist leaders and followers.

In examining this subject, we must begin from a foundational knowledge that interaction between the sexes is highly controlled at best and severely curtailed in the most fundamentalist sectors, again, such as the Wahhabists. As such, young men and women begin lives together in the case of arranged marriages with a very limited understanding of each other, in terms of gender. While it is understood that a young man and woman will enter into the bonds of matrimony at a certain time in their lives, often men know much more about their sisters and/or their mothers than they do about their wives, and often these relationships are much more impacting in their lives than a spousal relationship.

In the case of Khalayleh for instance, while in prison, though married at the time, he communicated often with his sisters and mother but rarely with his wife. His communications with his sisters (letters most often) were laced with poetry hinting at romantic ardor and longing.[13] There is no evidence that he ever entered into any incestuous relationships, but the writings indicate a much closer bond between him and his sisters, than between him and his wife.

At the height of his career as a terror leader, Khalayleh had earned a reputation as much more vicious, brutal. and cruel even than bin Laden. Most of his victims were other Muslims and included a large percentage of women and children. In later years, many people in his life had turned their backs on him due to this orchestration of the slaughter of so many innocent Jordanians and Muslims in the region.

Of note however are the different responses of two of his siblings, to his eventual death at the hands of American military forces.

"We anticipated he would be killed for a very long time," said one sibling, Sayel.

"We expected that he would be martyred, and hope that he joins other martyr's in heaven," said another.

The two responses are indicative of the vast array of opinions toward Islamic extremists and those who pursue terrorism in the name of Islamic purity. It is quite common for mothers of suicide bombers to be honored and proud of their children for pursuing such an act. They see their children as martyrs that will be rewarded in heaven and bring honor to their families on earth.

Khalayleh had over the course of his adulthood four wives and five children. It is instructive however that he spoke rarely of his wives but often of his sisters and his mother. It is also instructive that when he finally decided to leave Jordan, a year after his release from prison and begin a new life in Pakistan, he didn't take his wives; he took instead his mother.

The day Khalayleh and his mother turned up at the airport in Jordan, with passports and Pakistani visas in hand, the Mukabarat stopped them. They had no idea what Khalayleh was up to, but they weren't going to let him go without trying to find out. By law they could hold him up to three days without charges, but the fact was that in such a situation, the Mukabarat wasn't really bound by such. That said, following three days of questioning, all they could get from him was that he was going to Pakistan to become a bee farmer.

The irony here is that there is a high probability that he was telling the truth. Most people, even some experienced counterterrorism experts, in hindsight just assume that all these people, (people who one day would run vast terror organizations) always had well-thought-out plans in mind, though luckily most didn't work out. The reality is that, returning to the theme of this text, they are not a great deal different from most young people, in that they normally aren't sure about their path in life and normally have not given a lot of thought as to how it all would work out. In this particular case, one of the reasons the Mukabarat couldn't uncover any complicated plan that was to begin with Khalayleh leaving the country for Pakistan to Zarqa to become a bee farmer is that he probably had every intention to "leave the country for Pakistan, to become a bee farmer."

At any rate, following three days or so, he was allowed to board the plane, albeit alone. His mother had long since tired of the questioning and returned home to Zarqa, Jordan.

At this point, the Russians are a non-issue to any impacting extent, bin Laden is in Afghanistan and has begun isolated terrorist attacks against the US positions around that part of the world, Khalayleh has left for Pakistan (his ultimate goals undistinguishable for now), Mullah Mohammad Omar and his Taliban are slowly taking control of the country of Afghanistan, and Bill Clinton is completing his second term as President of the United States. Soon all these men's lives will intersect in a world-altering way.

We will return and pick up with the process in terms of Khalayleh, but for the time being, here, we will switch gears and examine the state of affairs in the United States. Record your timeline here, accordingly.

THE UNITED STATES OF AMERICA: A PLAYER IN THE PROCESS

Though this text is devoted primarily to the behind-the-scenes development of terror organizations such as Al Qaeda, ISIS, AQI (Al Qaeda in Iraq)
and others, we must consider that as the west, and principally the United
States, was paramount in terms of the enemies of these organizations, steps
taken by the United States strongly influenced "steps taken by these organizations." Politics in America as well as the activities of politicians and
decision makers in America had a great deal of effect on how the world
dealt with (or failed to deal with in some cases) these threats, which in turn
had a great deal of effect on the developmental courses of these groups.

In this period, Osama bin Laden is in Afghanistan and is actively
planning and carrying out (through his direction principally) attacks
against American interest in that part of the world. Bin Laden had already been identified as the driving force behind attacks on the USS Cole
in the harbor at Aden Yemen in 2000, as well as successful coordinated
attacks on the American embassies in Dar es-Salaam, Tanzania, and
Nairobi, Kenya, in August of 1998. Though this section is devoted to
America and American foreign policy toward these events, it is illumi-
nating to a point to understand bin Laden's personal objectives.

Bin Laden had declared full-scale war against America. Two years before, he had declared war on the United States; however, from his point of
view, though he hated America and everything America stood for, his
hatred for the Saudi royal family was far greater. One might ask under these
circumstances, why didn't he declare war against Saudi Arabia? Why didn't
he attack targets that were principally Saudi (he had directed the attack on
the US Marine barracks at Khobar Towers in Khobar, Saudi Arabia, but
analysts agree, his principal target wasn't Saudi Arabia; it was the American
marines housed there). Why the total focus on America as the enemy?

The authors agree with many analysts who assess his reasoning
thusly; Wahhabi fundamentalists like Osama bin Laden had long advocated for a return to the purity of Islam (Sharia) which in their mind
would bring a return to days of strength and power of Islam over all the
world's nations. Such had in fact been the case generations before. During
this earlier period in history, such prosperity and strength were exhibited
for the whole world to see, not in an Islamic nation but in the entire world.

Bin Laden thus reasoned that as long as America, the most powerful
nation in the world, wasn't challenged, the bin Laden/Wahhabist promise of a return to greatness that would accompany the return to the

purity of Islam would seem ineffective and little more than the ravings of religious purists. He had to bring down and humiliate America in the eyes of all who listened to him.

Bin Laden believed that for its lack of piety Allah would intervene to bring America to its knees. However, while Allah has his timetable, bin laden had his, and although he couldn't hope to do it by himself, as he had recently met with much success bringing people together to fight the Russians, he likely felt confident that the entire Sunni Muslim world would coalesce behind him to "speed" the will of Allah, proving conclusively that the message of Al Qaeda was a righteous one and totally aligned with the will of Allah.

It was in this time and in this scenario that the most powerful man in the world, President Bill Clinton, was being impeached for his dalliance with a young intern, Monica Lewinsky. A challenging mind game, and one a myriad of analysts the world over have contemplated in hindsight, is to speculate as to what America would have been able to accomplish in its war against terrorism and against Osama bin Laden, had President Clinton been more adept at controlling his libido. In reality however, it is safe to say, every decision President Clinton made during this time was filtered through the sieve of his political conundrum (in fairness, however, President George Bush, Clinton's successor, had other political considerations that helped or hindered follow-on decisions vis-a-vis Al Qaeda and the search for Osama bin Laden). A complete and accurate study of the development of terror groups such as Al Qaeda cannot be made unless these considerations are rolled into the mix.

When carrying out aggressive, defensive or offensive actions, America acts based upon moral, legal and internationally acceptable authority. Of equal importance however is the consideration of political will. With President Clinton, many analysts believe that "political will" trumped all other considerations.

It is safe to say, and to factor into this discussion, that Osama bin Laden had proven himself a legally acceptable target for American forces. He had not only declared his intentions, relative to declaration of war against America, he had also orchestrated and ordered the conduct of terrorist actions that had killed thousands of people mostly Americans, and America was in possession of all the necessary evidence in support.

Bin Laden had funded and ordered two attacks in Saudi Arabia targeting American forces, before his declaration of war against America in 1996. In 1998, he ordered two attacks against American embassies in Tanzania and Kenya killing hundreds, and of course, the 2000 attack against the USS Cole, killing 17 American soldiers; all this before the twin towers attacks on 9/11. We had the evidence and moral authority we needed to take him out.

What we didn't have was actionable intelligence, and political will in light of the fact that President Clinton was dealing with impeachment over the Monica Lewinsky affair prior to the 9/11 attacks of course. Actually, the lack of intelligence gave President Clinton a slight bit of political cover for refusing to order the killing of bin Laden. On at least three separate occasions, America came within minutes of ordering airstrikes against bin Laden and his people, only to have them called back over last minute snafus.

During these planned attacks, America was relying primarily on the intelligence of unproven Afghan assets on the ground in the vicinity of bin Laden's operational areas, as America had no viable reliable intelligence assets in operation in Afghanistan.[4] We just didn't have trained American intelligence operatives in the area and as such were hampered in these efforts. Such unreliability of agents ironically served to provide President Clinton and his staff additional support for last minute denial for operations. In fairness to President Clinton, the situation was far from optimal for "capture-kill" operations.

One airstrike on Tarnak Farms, where bin Laden was living in eastern Afghanistan, was canceled because satellite imagery indicated the possible presence of children.[4] On another, strikes on a bin Laden "bird hunting" party in the desert outside the farm area were canceled because there was a possibility that some members of the Saudi royal family were present.[4] There has been and will for years be much speculation that the 9/11 attacks could have been avoided were it not for President Clinton's sexual indiscretions.

In each of these cases, however, word of the attacks being rescinded reached bin Laden or his people and emboldened him and his followers. Bin Laden escalated his process and enhanced his stature by offering rewards on American officials each time America would announce a reward on him.

America's greatest concern at that time was of course Al Qaeda and Osama bin Laden. We were very dubious however about the potential for the Taliban to rise to the occasion and lead the country. That seemed to be the direction things were going; however, so we did what America does best, far too often; we took a "wait and see attitude." The only problem is that this "wait and see" attitude presented a huge problem that we are dealing with, still today.[2]

When the Russians left, there was an anticipated void in leadership, and every nation in the world that finds itself facing such a problem sees an accompanying rise in violence while factions fight to fill such a void.

Though many will argue the point, America does have a vested interest in controlling to an extent who will fill such voids around the world. The legitimacy of our interest comes in part in the assumption by the rest of the world that America is the leader of the free world. Being the leader too often means that we have to shoulder an unreasonably large part of the financial burden involved in seeing that a country that has survived a war is rebuilt. We are expected by the rest of the world to do this, and we normally try to fulfill that expectation. As such, we do what we can to influence the leadership and the choice of leaders.

In Afghanistan, however, we wanted to stay as far away from the situation as possible. We still remembered the embarrassing costly defeat in Vietnam and the world had just witnessed Russia's similar humiliation in this country. We had entered Vietnam at a time when another country (France) had just been defeated and routed from that nation. There was no way we were going to repeat the exact mistake in Afghanistan.

Since the Taliban seemed to be the best hope for stable leadership even though they had shown no intention of being "stable," we adopted a "hands-off" policy in hopes they would find their "heart" and become a strong benevolent leading force for the country.[5] In the long run, that didn't happen, and before long we saw the nation sink into sectarian and tribal warfare, the likes of which rivaled the brutality of the Russian occupation.

In short, as far as America's actions during this period, we were hesitant and our hesitancy, as is often the case, encouraged and emboldened our adversary. We will return to America's actions and how they contributed to the growth and actions of not only Al Qaeda but the Taliban and, in later years, the Islamic State.

KHALAYLEH, TALIBAN AND AL QAEDA: PUTTING THE BAND BACK TOGETHER

Adjust your timeline here, accordingly; in early 2000, bin Laden and his Al Qaeda followers were in eastern Afghanistan. The Taliban, indigenous to Afghanistan, was moving north across the country from its stronghold in Kandahar (southern Afghanistan). Khalayleh was in Pakistan but soon to leave there and go to Afghanistan to join forces with bin Laden.

Shortly after Khalayleh arrived in Pakistan, possibly trying to make his dream of becoming a bee farmer come true, the Pakistani government became leery of his presence in the country. Pakistan, during the Russian occupation of Afghanistan, had welcomed Islamic fighters (shooters) from all over the world, knowing full well that many if not most of them were potential trouble. The war was over however, and the government of Pakistan had turned its attention to national security. The presence of so many strong-willed Islamists from all over the Islamic world was troubling to say the least. Folks like Khalayleh were concerning for the government, so Pakistan began slowly inviting them to go back to wherever they came from.

Ahmad al-Khalayleh by this time had failed in his attempts to produce honey (it's still to this day unclear whether he actually wanted to lead such a life or was playing a game all along just to leave Jordan and get into Afghanistan to align with bin Laden).

We do know that before leaving Jordan, the Mukabarat had worn him down, and during the time they were maintaining such a tight rein on him, he had not been involved in insurgent or planning activities and he definitely had not been in contact with any of his old friends of like mind. Otherwise, he would have been re-arrested and jailed on severe suspicion. It is at least possible that he had been beaten down and possibly considered simply accepting his country the way it was or leaving to try to live a more normal life away from the constant pressure.[10]

At any rate, by this time, his Pakistani visa had expired so he was invited to leave. Whatever his thought process, he sought out Al Qaeda. A short trip west, across the border into Afghanistan, brought him fairly close to an area most people were aware of as "Al Qaeda country" in the vicinity of Tarnak farms where bin Laden's training camps were located. This area in east central Afghanistan was also close to the Tora Bora region, from which bin Laden was to exit Afghanistan never to return.

By this time in early 2000, Khalayleh had adopted the name Abu Musab al-Zarqawi (it was common, as it still is today for young Muslim men to change their name when they become involved with jihadist or terror-based groups).

> *Author's Note: From this point forward in the book, "Khalayleh" will be referred to as "Zarqawi."*

Soon after he arrived, he went straight to bin Laden's headquarters and begged an audience with the man. Bin Laden was skeptical of him and refused to meet with him (Zarqawi, it is said, was always boisterous, braggadocious, loudly proclaiming his piety and his zeal to fight, and such an attitude was off-putting for many. It is likely that his boisterous nature was a feint to cover for his lack of formal education and what he saw as inferior nature).

Bin Laden did order one of his top commanders to meet with the young man to see if there was any future in a relationship of some sort. They knew Zarqawi had strong connections among jihadists in Jordan and thought this might be helpful for recruitment purposes. Following the meeting, bin Laden's commander recommended that they keep Zarqawi around but not too close.

Zarqawi was given "start-up" funding and sent to the far northwest part of Afghanistan to a remote area to set up a recruitment and training site to bring people from Jordan. He left, having never yet met face to face with bin Laden (actually, though these two men had a somewhat contentious relationship for a number of years, no evidence exists that they ever actually met in person). Zarqawi set up a training camp in an area west of Herat close to the Iranian border, and for a while, was highly successful bringing men over from Jordan. At the time, Osama bin Laden was deep in the "war of words" with the United States (he had, by this time, officially declared war on the United States), in the process to some extent with the 9/11 operation, and dealing with requests from Mullah Mohammad Omar and his Taliban. He had little time to consider Zarqawi for any reason.

NOTES

1 List of Military Equipment Used by Mujahideen During Soviet –Afghan War. (n.d.). In *Wikipedia*. Retrieved May 23, 2020, from https://en.wikipedia.org/wiki/List_of_military_equipment_used_by_mujahideen_during_Soviet%E2%80%93Afghan_War. Accessed 23 May. 2020.
2 Rashid, A. (2010). *Taliban*. Yale University Press.
3 Britannica. (n.d.). Northern alliance: Afghani military organization. *Britannica*. Retrieved May 23, 2020, from https://www.britannica.com/topic/Northern-Alliance.
4 Coll, S. (2004). *Ghost wars: The secret history of the CIA*. Penguin Press.
5 Barfield, T. (2004). *Afghanistan: A cultural and political history*. Princeton University.
6 Nasr, V. (2006). *The Shia revival: How conflicts within Islam will shape the future*. W. W. Norton and Company Publishers.
7 Coll, S. (2018). *Directorate S: The C.I.A. and America's Secret Wars in Afghanistan and Pakistan*. Penguin Press.
8 J. Shroder, personal communication, May 30, 2020.
9 Trofimov, Y. (2008). *The siege of Mecca: The forgotten uprising in Islam's holiest shrine and the birth of al-Qaeda*. Anchor Publishing.
10 McCants, W. (2015). *The ISIS apocalypse: The history, strategy, and doomsday vision of the Islamic State*. St Martins Publishing.

11 Ansary, T. (2012). *Games without rules: The often interrupted history of Afghanistan*. Perseus Publishers.
12 Abu Musab al-Zarqawi. (n.d.). In *Wikipedia*. https://en.wikipedia.org/wiki/Abu_Musab_al-Zarqawi.
13 Warrick, J. (2015). *Black flags: The rise of ISIS*. Regan Arts.
14 Ghattas, K. (2020). *Black wave*. Headline Publishing Group.
15 Wright, L. (2006). *The terror years: From Al Qaeda to the Islamic State*. Knopf Publishing.
16 Weiss, M. (2015). *ISIS: Inside the army of terror*. Phaidon Publishers.
17 (2008). Al Qaeda use two Down's syndrome women to blow up 99 people in Baghdad markets. *MailOnline*. https://www.dailymail.co.uk/news/article-511678/AlQaeda-use-Downs-syndrome-women-blow-99-people-Baghdad-markets.html.
18 Weiss, M. (2015). *ISIS: Inside the army of terror*. Phaidon Publishers.

7

Meeting Key Players
Mullah Omar and the Taliban

MULLAH MOHAMMAD OMAR AND THE TALIBAN

During this same period, Mullah Omar and the Taliban were busy taking over the country. They had met with much success in the south, heavily populated by Pashtun tribes most of which were very supportive, as the Taliban was/is primarily Pashtun, but further north, they met resistance and were mired down fighting with the Northern Alliance (made up of its Tajik leader, Ahmad Shah Masood, Rashid Dostum and his Junbish e-Milli, Ata Mohammad Noor's Jamiat e-Islami as well as Mohammad Mohaqiq, leader of the Hazara, Hezb e-Wahdat) from the north and east, and Gulbuddin Hekmatyar leader of the Hezb-e Islami party from the northwest part of the country, each of whom had a drastically different idea of who and what would lead the country and who would be the first to set foot in Kabul as conqueror.

It is important here to understand the relationship dynamics between Mullah Omar, bin Laden and the United States, and how these dynamics played out to manipulate the landscape in Afghanistan both before and after 9/11. In doing this, we'll step back a little to the point when bin Laden returned to Afghanistan. At this time, Mullah Omar's Taliban was in its infancy but gaining strength quickly. Omar was strengthening through his ground contacts and the efforts of his Taliban fighters by pursuing a type of "hearts and minds" (this would very soon morph into a "my way or death" strategy) program, but he was also establishing relationships with world leaders.

Keep in mind that now that Russia had exited the country, the world could breathe a sigh of relief. Most leaders around the world, especially the Middle East, just wanted stability in Afghanistan, and they really didn't care who brought it or, for that matter, who was in charge. Omar seemed a likely choice since he'd already begun the process and seemed at the time to have the strength to do it.[1] The world, however, was still a little leery of his demeanor and was just hoping he wouldn't do exactly what he eventually did: go around the country cutting people's limbs off and stoning women for adultery. In the end, everyone just kept their head in the sand hoping he'd change his leadership style.

For his part, Omar just wanted the world to leave him alone so he could accomplish the mission of gaining complete control of the country and establishing an Islamic fundamentalist style sharia-run nation (keep in mind, this mission, an Allah-inspired one, has never changed and will resume if and when the Taliban is ever given a strong power-sharing role in the country, as a result of treaty). The last thing he wanted was intervention by the United States, and he feared just such an intervention from his agreeing to shelter Osama bin Laden and Al Qaeda (as we will see, bin Laden worked hard to assure Omar he would be "a good visitor," a promise that of course he had no intentions of keeping).

Along comes bin Laden and his Al Qaeda followers asking for a homeland to begin "their" work, which he assured Omar would not bring down the wrath of America on his country. Bin Laden and his people, due to pressure from the United States, had already been evicted from two countries including his own homeland. Why did Omar invite him to come in and stay? The answer is simple and straightforward; Omar was proud and stubborn and extremely confident, and he was not going to allow the United States to "bully" him.

The United States, on the other hand, was to an extent, obstinate and authoritative and felt that since they had spent so much money defending Afghanistan against the Russians, they had a right to demand certain favors from Omar. When the United States demanded that Omar not give sanctuary to bin Laden, the act was tantamount to a parent telling a stubborn kid not to sneak any more cookies from the cookie jar.

Many have speculated that if America had made its wishes known in a different tone, Omar likely would not have harbored bin Laden and crew. Interviews with some of the early Taliban members who were close

104

to Omar reveal a sort of distant relationship between Omar and bin Laden in the beginning. Omar was practical and not unintelligent. When bin Laden asked for safe haven, Omar knew it would likely bring drama down upon him (exactly what it eventually did), and he didn't want to deal with that, especially since bin Laden's objectives were international in nature and Omar's were not and still aren't.[1]

For his part, bin Laden was highly intelligent and knew it would take a little sweetening to get Omar to support him, even before the United States had issued its proclamation. To accomplish this, he ordered his construction company to build a complete home for Omar and his family in the base of a mountain just outside the Omar complex a few miles southeast of Kandahar (this structure was never completed having been destroyed when America entered the country). One of the authors of this text in 2003, while living in this former home of Mullah Omar, walked among the (never fully completed) lavish tunnels and rooms of the cave which is complete with a bronze plate over the entrance, proclaiming that it was built by the bin Laden Construction Company. Several of the former Taliban members also alluded to marriages between Omar and one of bin Laden's daughters and bin Laden and one of Omar's daughters, as a time honored way to seal the relationship (Figure 7.1).

Mullah Omar was stubborn, however, and he was not going to allow anyone to tell him how to run the organization he had formed. Such, in his mind it is assumed, would be tantamount to Allah himself taking advice from others (Figure 7.2).

The fact is Mullah Omar had proclaimed himself Amir al-Mu'minin; in short, the leader of all Islam, some say, the next best thing to Mohammad himself.[1] He did this in the beginning of his formation of the Taliban, in his home base and ancestral home of Kandahar, and at a time when the people all expected great things to come from the reign of the Taliban. He also did it in a highly theatrical manner that few others would have been able to pull off.

He retrieved a cloak, said to have belonged to the Prophet Mohammad himself, that had been kept locked away in The Shrine of the Cloak. Donning this cloak with what some said was a slight theatrical flourish, he proclaimed himself, "basically in charge."

From that day forward, Omar seemed to adopt the air of a deity, and the United States wasn't the only entity he shunned and refused to acquiesce too, in any way. Pakistan had encouraged him and supported his rule since his religious zeal and philosophy was similar to theirs,

Figure 7.1 Author, Garner, in black shirt, standing inside one of the tunnels in the bin Laden Construction Company structure designed to be an escape shelter for Omar in the event of American bombing.
(Source: Author's personal photo).

but even they had trouble sending their emissaries to meet personally with the man.[1]

Omar even demonstrated this air of independence and stubbornness against other national Taliban leaders. When Omar announced to the world his intentions to dynamite the famous monumental statues of Gautama Buddha carved into the side of a cliff in the Bamiyan valley in the Hazarajat region of central Afghanistan, some of his command level people argued against it for fear it would do exactly what it did, that is, turn much of the world against the Taliban.[2]

The famous anti-Soviet fighter Jalaluddin Haqqani, at that time the head of the Haqqani Taliban network, it is said, attempted to reason with Omar on the destruction of the statues, but it was too late. By that time, too many people around the world had, assuming the role of the afore-mentioned parent, demanded that he leave the artifacts alone.

106

Figure 7.2 Author at entrance of Mullah Omar's Bunker. Sign over the entrance commemorates the structure as built by bin Laden Construction Company. (Source: Author's personal photo).

When America invaded Afghanistan following 9/11, one of the first things we did in an attempt to kill the leadership of the Taliban was to bomb the Mullah Omar compound in Kandahar. Omar and his family at that time however had escaped to Pakistan, approximately 70 miles to the east (Figure 7.3).

American forces later rebuilt part of the compound and turned it into a Special Forces/intelligence operations center. One of this text's authors lived and operated out of the complex in 2003 and later in 2005. A road leading from Kandahar to the complex splits at the entrance and circles the compound which is complete with several buildings and its own Mosque.

Curiously, at the front of the entrance where the road splits sits an inoperable fountain constructed of plaster and wire, designed to look very much like an old dying tree with a pool at its base. At one time the water ran from the limbs of the tree into the pool. Some of the older

(a)

(b)

Figure 7.3 (a) Inside Mullah Omar's ruined compound in Kandahar. (b) Author Garner standing on some rubble of the compound in Kandahar. The compound was later converted to a base for Special Operations.
(Source: Author's personal photos).

Figure 7.4 Inoperable fountain at the entrance of Mullah Omar's compound built to his specifications, some say to replicate a scene from a movie he had once seen.
(Source: Author's personal photo).

members of the neighborhood said that Omar had at one time viewed a western-style horror movie in which such a tree was the focus and had the tree fountain constructed not long afterward (Figure 7.4).

THE TALIBAN MOVES; THE WORLD SIMPLY WATCHES

As stated, no other nations wanted to be involved in Afghanistan. It had proven many times to be most assuredly *The Graveyard of Empires,* as its long-held nickname implies. To be fair, some in the US Congress wanted to continue involvement there until the country had recovered somewhat, but the rest of the country just didn't buy into it. Russia had been defeated and humiliated, and politically, that's all we (America) were interested in.

While it is true, we hoped Omar would be a benevolent leader, but we did little more at the time than "hope." Our only interest in the country at that time was bin Laden's presence there. Though our intelligence agencies and the FBI had competing interests in what he was doing, few people argued against the assertion that he was going to be trouble. He had already proven his intent to be "just that."

Saudi Arabia's intentions vis-à-vis the Taliban were more intrinsic and perhaps slightly narcissistic. It was very obvious that The House of Saud was intent on living vicariously through the Taliban (the Taliban's intent of instituting "true Islam" and harsh punishment for those who didn't comply, which being synonymous with Wahhabism fit the desired outcome of the Saudi Royal family though they didn't themselves want to be seen as imposing such on another sovereign nation).

As such Saudi Arabia was one of only three nations who recognized the Taliban as the legitimate ruler of Afghanistan.[1] The religious ideology of the Taliban mirrored Wahhabism in almost every way, allowing the royal family to see just how things could be had they not decided that a closer relationship with the west would make life more comfortable for them. Their involvement, however, extended to no more than funneling money into the country to assist Mullah Omar.

As far as gathering intelligence on bin Laden, though we had been using some local individuals, that wasn't working out well, and we certainly weren't going to put American intelligence operations on the ground there. The closest formal operations were in Pakistan, and as it worked out, we were often at odds with the intelligence services in that country. The country of Pakistan was and still is more in alignment with the religious ideology of the Taliban and Al Qaeda (fundamentalist Islam) than we would like. We decided our best bet to keep really close tabs on bin Laden and use the best opportunity to, at some point, take him out. We were working closely with the Northern Alliance, specifically at that time (before his assassination) with the leader Ahmad Shah Masood (Figure 7.5).

For America, the plan ostensibly was simple. We would provide Masood with the resources he needed, to a point, to fight the Taliban, resources that incidentally would include radios encrypted to communicate directly with Langley, to pass encrypted intelligence on Al Qaeda. As he pressed his war against the Taliban, his men would also monitor the movements and activities of bin Laden's Al Qaeda. Sometimes it worked and sometimes it didn't, but it did keep our involvement in Afghanistan to a minimum. Remember, we not only had a reluctant

Figure 7.5 Ahmad Shah Masood, the Tajik leader of the Northern Alliance Consortium.[3]

congress back home, but a President of the United States who was in no position to take political risks, due to the Lewinsky situation. The problem with this arrangement is that Masood didn't share our concern for the activities of Al Qaeda, and he had a full plate dealing with the Taliban (though history would prove, he should have been more

111

concerned). As a result, other than funneling some money to the Northern Alliance, we just watched and waited for an opportunity in which the President could/would act.

In the interim, the Taliban was getting stronger and bin Laden's people were in various stages of planning the attacks of 9/11. Of note, during this period of time is the fact that there was very little involvement between Omar and bin Laden, and it is highly likely that Mullah Omar had no idea who Musab Zarqawi was, and even though Zarqawi would at some point be the "face of terrorism" in the Middle East. Osama bin Laden had probably forgotten all about Zarqawi at this time, as well.

> *As a side note: at the writing of this text, the United States signed a peace deal with the Taliban for our troops to withdraw from Afghanistan. This is a highly anticipated process and has been years in the making. The details include a United States withdrawal from Afghanistan within 14 months of signing the treaty. The deal, to a degree, officially recognizes the Taliban as a legitimate political entity in the country. Every effort is being taken to assure the Taliban does not return to its former mission of subjugating the country through brutality. The agreement states that the Taliban are not to let any other group have control in the area, that is, Al Qaeda, ISIS, etc. A subsequent attack on a maternity ward in Kabul, on behalf of ISIS, in which over 20 mothers and newborn babies were killed, is putting the deal in jeopardy. Of interest, however, is the push from the United States and the Afghan government to obtain concessions from the Taliban leadership, which assure, they will never harbor or provide safe haven to any terrorist organization. This obvious concentration of effort is being made with the memories of the presence of Al Qaeda, in mind. Of consideration, however, is that the Taliban never intended to harbor Al Qaeda or any other terror group for that matter, from its inception. As we have stated earlier in this book, bin Laden cajoled and forced his presence in the country on Mullah Omar and was successful in large part as a result of the American "demand" that Omar refuse him refuge and safe haven (stated earlier, Omar's independence and ego forced him to dismiss a "demand"). The Taliban did not then desire or encourage, nor has it ever desired or encouraged, the presence of any other organized group such as Al Qaeda in Afghanistan. The Taliban is a perfect example of a*

regional, domestic terror group in that they never intended to act outside the borders of Afghanistan. Such a move (harboring another terror organization) would be detrimental to their efforts of being the leader and most formidable force in Afghanistan with an eventual, "deity ordained" mission of establishing a thoroughly fundamental Islamic, nation controlled by shariah. Harboring or offering safe haven to some other group, especially if they were going to bring outside pressure on you, as did Al Qaeda, is the last thing the Taliban want to do, especially at a time when the United States was planning to withdraw forces. Exacting such a promise or pledge from the Taliban leadership, especially if a quid pro quo is offered, is definitely a "red herring" effort.

NOTES

1 Rashid, A. (2010). *Taliban*. New Haven, CT: Yale University Press.
2 Buddhas of Bamyan. (n.d.). In *Wikipedia*. Retrieved May 31, 2020, from https://en.wikipedia.org/wiki/Buddhas_of_Bamyan.
3 Ahmad Shah Massoud. (n.d.). In *Wikipedia*. https://en.wikipedia.org/wiki/Ahmad_Shah_Massoud.

8

Osama bin Laden; Mullah Mohammad Omar; Their Focus during This Period

Osama bin Laden during this time had very little to do with the Taliban. He was almost assuredly funneling some operational funds to them, but other commanders in his operation handled that.

Bin Laden himself had "bigger fish to fry."

It is important to understand the focus of these two men and their operations. Mullah Mohammad Omar, the supreme leader of the Taliban, had no visible interest in establishing the caliphate. He was obviously not opposed to the idea of being a devout and committed Muslim, but his principal focus was Afghanistan. There is no indication that Omar was unintelligent, but few would attempt to argue that he was "worldly." Omar and the Taliban were ("are" in the case of the Taliban) a classic example of a regional/domestic terror organization. In short, they couldn't care less what happened outside the nation of Afghanistan. Of course, all this changed to a degree after 9/11, but even today, at the writing of this text, the existing Taliban organization and leadership are not interested in what happens outside the country as long as their "national goals and interests" remain intact and unmolested.

Al Qaeda and Osama bin Laden, on the other hand, were/are the polar opposite. Bin Laden's desire to establish an Islamic state (caliphate), in which whole world was converted to Islam and the world's people were governed by *shariah*, was very obviously an international goal and effort.

Bin Laden proceeded with this effort as Omar did with his, and the two men rarely interacted.

In hindsight, however, it is likely that Omar didn't want to be too closely connected to Al Qaeda. Some would contend that he always knew bin Laden was going to bring down a hammer on him and his household at some point in the future. Bin Laden's effort to construct a safe haven in the base of the mountain outside Omar's compound south of Kandahar (discussed and illustrated earlier in this text) was very obviously an attempt to mitigate any concerns Omar had. Bin Laden was likely counting on Omar's ignorance of logical reactions on the part of the United States to the Al Qaeda operations. He knew that the United States wouldn't let a mountain fortress keep them from capturing or killing Omar and probably him as well, once he launched more ambitious operations, but Omar probably did not foresee this. The cave complex was little more than a "feel-good" measure.

As the Taliban continued in its effort to take total control of the country, bin Laden continued in his effort to fund and coordinate future Al Qaeda operations, and Zarqawi continued recruiting and training operatives and fighters for Al Qaeda, at his complex in northwest Afghanistan, outside Herat.

WHAT WAS AMERICA DOING

Keep in mind that we're discussing a period before 9/11. The irony is that in America, most in the field of counterterrorism, to the extent it existed at the time, knew something was going to happen, but they just didn't have the details and enough information to act decisively, and unfortunately, the two premier agencies, the FBI and the CIA, were not cooperating. As a matter of fact, they were intentionally operating at cross-purposes.

Bin Laden had already orchestrated terrorist operations around the Middle East and Africa, and there was little question that he was in control of these events. As stated, to complicate issues, the relationship between the FBI and the CIA, the two agencies most responsible for dealing with acts of terrorism at the time, was strained to say the least due in part to the vast differences in their respective missions. The FBI was and is a law enforcement agency charged with keeping America safe by investigating crimes and potential crimes, identifying the perpetrators and putting them behind bars. The CIA is responsible for collecting and analyzing information, which often means identifying the perpetrators (bad guys), allowing them to continue operations and simply watching them in order to collect more information. As far as the CIA is concerned, once a bad guy has been identified and is being watched, if he's taken off the street through arrests, the flow of new information/intelligence potentially gained from him ends. To put it mildly, they were not on the same sheet of music as far as bin Laden is concerned, and they definitely were not sharing information.

From the standpoint of the CIA, if they had shared information with the FBI, their source of data and future intelligence would end. Of course, there were the associated political and "turf war" implications as well, both agencies being somewhat mildly, egregiously, political. From a standpoint of politics, of course there was the issue of the Monica Lewinsky/President Bill Clinton situation and the President's pending impeachment hearings. It was just a bad time all around for America's safety and security.

Ironically, the most knowledgeable terror investigator, FBI Special Agent in charge of counterterrorism efforts, John P. O'Neill was killed in the Twin Towers on 9/11. O'Neill had been at the point of the spear in the FBI's effort to thwart that very operation. Due to personal indiscretions, he had been determined to have violated several rules within the agency and had tendered his resignation and left the agency days before the attack. He had accepted a position at the Twin Towers as head of security. His first day on the job was September 11, 2001. He was 49 years old[1] (Figure 8.1).

As is the case, with most law enforcement and intelligence organizations at times like this, the real productivity and cooperation came in at the ground level with the people who were actually doing the job. Bin Laden was the focus of intelligence efforts inside Afghanistan, but the actual gathering of intelligence, a highly technical, complicated, difficult process at best, was being done by folks who in many cases didn't even have a high school degree and couldn't read or write, namely, the assets of the Northern Alliance, specifically Ahmad Shah Masood's men. This was obviously *not* an ideal situation.

In short, America was simply hanging on, hoping for a break, a break that never came. In the meantime, Omar, bin Laden and Zarqawi were all seeing various levels of success.

Figure 8.1 FBI agent John P. O'Neill.

AN ANNOYING MOSQUITO

For Osama bin Laden, America seemed more of an annoyance; though he had identified America and the west as the targets of his global jihad, he either wasn't concerned about their ongoing efforts to capture him, or he felt highly secure in his seclusion. He was continually granting interviews with major news organizations (this was obviously a move to magnify his persona and further establish his position as a worldwide Islamic leader) albeit from the safety and security of his home turf, in and around Tora Bora in east central Afghanistan, in the vicinity of Khost Province (the stronghold and ancestral home of Taliban commander of the Haqqani Taliban network, Jalaluddin Haqqani).

Bin Laden further tweaked the noses of America by boldly issuing death threats against the leaders of the CIA and intentionally offering larger rewards for them than those America had placed upon him. Bin Laden, in hindsight, was being seriously naive but at the time it seemed to the world that he was in control and America was little more than an annoying mosquito. This miscalculation, on his part, almost assuredly emboldened him in his support for, and coordination of, the events of 9/11.

Osama bin Laden's long-term objective was a global Islamic state and dominance of the world by Wahhabist-style Islam, and he was still motivated to a degree by his opposition to the royal family, but in the interim, he continued to rant about a war with America. Eschatologically speaking, the worldwide dominance of Islam will be preceded by a war, similar to Armageddon in Christianity, and this war will take place in the Middle East in Northern Iraq, in a location called Dabiq (ISIS in later years used this city of Dabiq as a rallying cry for recruitment).

It is conceivable that bin Laden was intent on escalating the process in pursuance of his long-term objectives. It should be understood in this light that bin Laden was by definition a megalomaniac, and many such individuals within religious structures are driven toward ending the world, confident in the assumption on their part that they themselves are "deity ordained" to bring this to pass.

Osama bin Laden did work closer with Mohammad Omar and the Taliban on one occasion to rid them of a powerful enemy leader in the Northern Alliance, Tajik leader Ahmad Shah Masood. He sent two Arabic suicide operatives, posing as Arab news reporters, to gain access to Masood under the guise of conducting an interview. During the first few minutes of the interview, they detonated explosives hidden in the camera, mortally wounding Masood. This happened two days before the attacks of 9/11.[2]

Other than this, however, the Taliban and Al Qaeda followed different objectives. On September 11, 2001, bin Laden was in his headquarters at Tora Bora, by all accounts, Mullah Omar was at home in Kandahar, and Musab Zarqawi was at his jihadist training camp outside Herat in northwestern Afghanistan.

THE AFTERMATH OF 9/11

Approximately one month had passed between the Al Qaeda attacks of 9/11 and actual "boots on the ground" in Afghanistan (members of initial invasion by 5th Special Forces Group to link with the Northern Alliance fighters). The events involved in those 30 days are both informative and crucial to the state of Islamic extremist terrorism today. Of equal importance however are the events that occurred before the 9/11 attacks. This section will deal with American movement and the background involved, as well as the actions of bin Laden, Omar and Zarqawi beginning shortly before the attacks, continuing to our invasion of Iraq. We will discuss the assumed reasoning behind these moves as well as how each affected the other. Much of this is slightly redundant, but it is designed to bring the student of this era up to a shared understanding of what was occurring behind the scenes, based on logic and the evaluations of experts who studied the actions. Since this text is designed to encourage independent thought and logic, some highly educated assumptions will be put forward. The reader is free to use the same basic data and come to his or her own educated conclusions.

WHY DID AMERICA NOT TAKE OUT THE TERRORIST LEADER, OSAMA BIN LADEN, BEFORE 9/11?

Following the attacks of 9/11, multiple hearings and reviews were launched in the US Congress. Fingers were pointed in several directions in seemingly "hindsight-fueled" attempts to blame. Such processes, ripe for misuse by those involved, are necessary and are performed on a regular basis in the US military. Euphemistically referred to as "after action reviews" (AARs), they are designed to explore and make use of lessons learned, in order to avoid mistakes in future operations. They are not processes designed to blame, although when conducted by the un-initiated, such as those with political motives, they can devolve to such.

Post 9/11 reviews often did this. There were serious mistakes made, some for political reasons and some inadvertent and innocent, but "mistakes" all the same, and mistakes we should strive never to make again. Official reports conducted at the time concluded that the lack of communication between agencies was to blame for the United States being ill-prepared for 9/11. It was also at this time, under the new Bush Administration, that the Department of Homeland Security (DHS) was created with a mission to focus solely on the national landscape and safety and security of our country.[3]

While our country was spending money post-9/11 on increasing security, Al Qaeda was celebrating the costly damage they had wrought on America. We were reacting just as they had hoped. By draining our economy and causing Americans temporarily, to live in fear and panic, they had seemingly scored a victory. Terrorist groups often emphasize the importance of attacking a nation's economy as another method in which to bring down that country, and the fact is the tactic works.

While other countries (such as Israel) focus on HUMINT (human intelligence) as a method to halt terrorism (Israel uses operatives at their airports to watch individuals and take note of their body language and behavior, a highly cost-effective tactic), the United States, post 9/11, resorted to high-tech, expensive maneuvers (e.g., body scanners, x-ray machines) in an attempt to keep our nation safe.

The year preceding the attacks of 9/11 was politically charged for several reasons. President Bill Clinton was replaced by President George Bush. President Bush's election was contentious due to the close ballot count and the era of "hanging chads." The political atmosphere just wasn't ripe for taking out a threat like bin Laden, especially since no one could actually put a finger on who and where, and as stated, the FBI and CIA were working basically against each other. We knew bin Laden was a threat, but there was no clear all-encompassing view on what his next move was, or how he should be handled. As a result, the perpetrators of the 9/11 attacks were allowed to continue with their plans.

Note, this was before the advent of the Department of Homeland Security which has greatly improved the chain of communication between agencies. At this time, as stated earlier, the two agencies most involved with actors associated with bin Laden, the FBI and the CIA, were far from sharing information.

To be fair, President Clinton did acquiesce to two halfhearted attempts to kill bin Laden in the weeks before he left office, but his actions were still extremely hampered and controlled by political issues, and the attempts were either thwarted or simply too little, too late. In the minds of most military analysts, these actions likely did more harm than good.

BIN LADEN, OMAR, ZARQAWI: WHAT DID THEY DO FOLLOWING THE ATTACKS

Ironically, Mullah Mohammad Omar and his Taliban received the brunt of America's response to 9/11, and it is highly likely that Omar had no idea the attacks were even being planned. As stated earlier in this text, Omar and bin Laden were pursuing different objectives, and they didn't communicate often. They did share one particularly fatal flaw, albeit for different reasons; they believed themselves safe from American retaliation.

Osama bin Laden allowed national media to film him celebrating the mass destruction brought on by 9/11. He was probably comfortable in the seclusion of the Tora Bora area, but beyond that, he had openly taunted America for weeks preceding the attacks, going so far as to declare war on the United States. Our response to this point, as detailed, had been muted.

Bin Laden likely didn't understand the domestic political back and forth in the states and didn't realize that the sense of security it offered him was temporary and false one. He did see the reality however; he was intentionally, and for his own reasons, antagonizing the most powerful country in the world, and we were doing virtually nothing about it. He knew, no doubt, that we would respond, but he probably figured President Bush would deal diplomatically with the Saudi Royals and with Omar.

Mullah Omar had not the higher formal education that bin Laden had. He, like Zarqawi, was an apt leader of men, but he seemingly didn't have a grasp of international matters and, for that matter, didn't care. It is likely that he thought, since he personally had nothing to do with the 9/11 attacks, and since the whole world to this point had placed their hopes in the illusion that he would morph into a benevolent leader, even turning a blind eye to the Taliban-orchestrated destruction of the Buddhist towers in Bamyan Province, he would escape consequences.

Omar probably felt that he was safe from any retribution over the actions of bin Laden and Al Qaeda. He even went so far as to counter President Bush's demands to hand over bin Laden, stating in response, "show me proof that bin Laden was involved." Ironically, even though highly deserved for reasons other than 9/11, the Taliban suffered the brunt of America's response to the Al Qaeda 9/11 attacks.

As America invaded Afghanistan and began, primarily through targeted airstrikes, assisting the Northern Alliance in defeating and virtually driving the Taliban out of Afghanistan for a time, bin Laden and the top Al Qaeda commanders quietly slipped out of Afghanistan into Pakistan.

A few Al Qaeda fighters were killed in the eventual fighting at Tora Bora, but most escaped.

NOTES

1 John P. O'Neill. (n.d.). In *Wikipedia*. Retrieved June 1, 2020, from https://en.wikipedia.org/wiki/John_P._O%27Neill.
2 Wright, L. (2016). *The terror years: From Al Qaeda to the Islamic State*. New York, NY: Knopf Publishing.
3 Homeland Security. (n.d.). Creation of the Department of Homeland Security. https://www.dhs.gov/creation-department-homeland-security.

9

Abu Musab Zarqawi

Author's Note: Most Americans, even those not yet born in 2001, can tell you who Osama bin Laden was. They may not know the minute details of his life, but they know who he was. That said, few could tell you who Abu Musab Zarqawi was. The irony is that Zarqawi was feared more by those who knew him, than bin Laden. Bin Laden himself was even somewhat afraid of the level of carnage Zarqawi was intent on unleashing on the world. For the student of international terrorism and the nuances and backstories, this section is extremely important. Learn who this man was. There are and will continue to be others who strive to be the next Zarqawi.

The American invasion of Afghanistan following the attacks of 9/11 actually served as a springboard of sorts for Zarqawi. He and his men in their training camp in Herat were really out of the loop, as to the 9/11 attacks, even more than Mullah Omar and the Taliban were. When it became clear that the Americans were coming, no one communicated with Zarqawi as to what he should do. He was sort of left out to dry. Up until this point, he was never really part of the Al Qaeda inner circle, and the fact is bin Laden probably still probably didn't know who he was.

That would all change soon, and change drastically.

Zarqawi didn't really know what he should do at this point but he was certain of one thing; he wanted to fight the Americans albeit when he was capable and when his men were ready. They weren't ready in Afghanistan, and besides, in Afghanistan, Zarqawi wasn't in a position to join in and help anyone. It is highly likely that he also knew the Taliban would be no match for the Americans and along with Al Qaeda, would be easily defeated. Staying in Afghanistan was a losing strategy for him and he knew that.

Though Zarqawi was uneducated and illiterate in many ways (his mother even swore he wasn't smart enough to be a leader of any group, let alone a group of jihadists), he had a strategic, analyst's mindset. He had the ability to make highly accurate predictions of his enemies' next moves, and the predictions were based on a sophisticated type of logic. Many warring leaders throughout history have possessed this uncanny ability while being unsophisticated in all other ways. Zarqawi predicted to his men, during this period, that America would, as a result of the determination of President Bush to go after Iraq's President Saddam Hussain, be in Iraq within the year. For this reason, he took his men to Northern Iraq. His prediction, of course, turned out to be true.

MUSAB ZARQAWI IN NORTHERN IRAQ: A LITTLE FISH IN A BIG POND

At the beginning of this text, the authors explained that much of what we write is conjecture, albeit based on much experience and knowledge of the subject matter, and in many cases, the actual characters we explore themselves. Dr. Garner is a PhD psychologist as well, and throughout the process of preparing this narrative, we have had a practicing psychologist on hand for consultation. Maeghin Alarid-Hughes is, in turn, a much experienced counterterrorism expert and a teacher/trainer of many practitioners both in and outside the military.

We say this to explain that certain areas of the text are by necessity based on highly supported conjecture. The actual facts surrounding these individuals are simply few and much debated, among professionals. Such is absolutely the case with Abu Musab al-Zarqawi. The summations we use with Zarqawi as well as the other terrorist figures, however, are heavily researched and based on proven related data.

Zarqawi, following his religious awakening as an adolescent, had an unusual zeal and desire to "fight the infidel" when and where that could be accomplished. His desire for martyrdom, "shahadat," from his early years had waned a bit by this point, likely because he had seen himself as an exceptional leader, capable of greater victories for Allah, alive.

When Zarqawi left Jordan following his release from prison and found himself in Afghanistan, he latched on to bin Laden and Al Qaeda as his best shot at fulfilling his destiny. In Jordan, he was much like any other lost pre/post adolescent. He likely knew that he had a special gift for jihad, but he didn't know how to put it into action. The only thing he knew for sure was that he wouldn't do it in Jordan.

A few of his followers, who had been released about the same time he had, lost their zeal for jihad and all the related risks. Like any other normal person being given a second chance, when they had initially assumed they'd die in prison, they weren't going to risk it.

His mentor Maqdisi was much like most of the firebrand fundamentalist mullahs and teachers of the period; they saw their role as encouraging younger men to sacrifice themselves for a cause they themselves felt much more comfortable, foisting on others to put in practice. In short, he (Maqdisi) went home to his wife and went about putting his life back together. Zarqawi, still full of the jihadist spirit, was basically alone, save for those he had recruited to join him in the Al Qaeda-funded training camp in northern Afghanistan.

Upon leaving Jordan, he may have fully intended to try to live a quiet life as a beekeeper in Pakistan, but even if this were the case, there was never much of a chance that he'd be successful at it. The Pakistani government obviously agreed, and Zarqawi soon found himself knocking on bin Laden's door.

Again, with the lack of connections and being fairly unknown in the community of terrorists and jihadists, bin Laden was his best and likely only choice for success. Of course, he had to convince bin Laden of this, and the best he could do at the time was to get a stipend to set his training camp at Herat.

When the attacks of 9/11 were followed by an American invasion of Afghanistan, and the Taliban had been, for the time being, routed, and bin Laden had fled the country, Zarqawi once again found himself alone, save for his newly recruited followers. He had gained a great deal of confidence however and may have actually seen the situation as an opportunity. Many analysts feel that it was around this time that Zarqawi made up his mind that the remainder of his life and his best chance for success and martyrdom, a "martyrdom" that few could even imagine, awaited him in northeast Iraq.[1]

Though he was unsophisticated and had little formal education, his instincts were often correct. He saw himself a leader and destined for greatness the way many with such visions of grandeur will. His greatness would come in the form of martyrdom, a martyrdom, however, that followed a lengthy battle with the infidels, as told in the Quran. The infidels of course were the Americans. To do this, he had to meet the

Americans on a battlefield chosen by him and in proximity to the fields of "Armageddon," as prophesied in the Quran; in this case, Dabiq.

Here his instincts directed him to northern Iraq. He knew the Americans would soon be there. He surmised this through an almost eerie analytical ability and a healthy dose of the aforementioned leader's instincts. He knew President Bush had been pushing heavily for American military involvement against Saddam Hussain in Iraq, and he also knew that the Americans would fairly easily rout the Taliban. Upon this evidence and while the Americans were busily sealing what they saw as a victory in Afghanistan, he took his men to northern Iraq. There, he proclaimed, they would meet the Americans on the battlefield.

ZARQAWI IN NORTHERN IRAQ: THE EARLY DAYS

When Musab Zarqawi and his men arrived in northern Iraq, they found themselves to be very little fish in a fairly large pond, surrounded by various jihadist groups led by various would-be leaders, each of whom no doubt saw themselves the next Osama bin Laden, now that few people knew where he (bin Laden) was or even if he were still alive. Zarqawi, much to his chagrin, made an almost unnoticed appearance. Zarqawi and his men initially aligned themselves with Ansar al Islam, a group made up of Sunni and Kurdish fighters, (note: ten years later, Ansar would dissolve and align with Islamic State of Iraq, the group founded by Zarqawi).

Though all these groups respected and, to an extent, revered Al Qaeda, primarily as a result of the attacks of 9/11 and the fact that Al Qaeda was so well funded, most of them maintained their independence. Curiously, Zarqawi did not initially proclaim his connection with bin Laden. It is possible that he intended, even at that early stage, to upstage the Al Qaeda leader, by declaring himself and his organization an independent group.

Zarqawi knew what he had to do however, and soon, he was making a name for himself among the local jihadists who migrated to this little enclave from all over the Muslim world. Zarqawi quickly began forging ties between Pakistan, Algeria and Morocco, raising money and gaining support from like-minded Islamists the world over. It was inevitable that he would also begin building local control. As a leader and organizer, in spite of his brutality and cruelty, his capabilities had to have been recognized and respected. Military analysts, trained to look objectively across the battlefield, recognized this and soon would realize the magnitude of it.

There were basically two groups of people in this area, vastly different in culture and appearance, but committed to the same objectives. These objectives bound them and superseded their differences. The more local Kurdish fighters intent on exacting revenge on Saddam Hussain, and his (Hussain's) people who had, within the past few short months, killed, through chemical poisoning, more people than had been killed at any point in history in this manner. They (the Kurds) were not as educated and so-phisticated as their Arab associates and complained loudly over the Islamist restrictions placed upon their daily lives (these Kurds, though devout Sunni Muslims, were far from fundamentalist and, in their homeland, resented the imposition of the Arabs who demanded they live their lives to Islamist standards). Whenever groups of jihadists gather, or find themselves in proximity to one another (through the male desire to demonstrate dom-inance or prominence), they initially strive to demonstrate their "purity." Once this has been established, the scale shifts quickly to the use of cruelty to establish their standards of behavior and demand the same from all present.

"They forced our women to wear the body covering burqa, to the fields when they go to attend the sheep herds," the local Kurdish men complained.

The ties that bound them, however, were much stronger. It is likely as well that the locals feared reprisals from their Arab counterparts, if they resisted these restrictions. Zarqawi's people were already gaining a reputation for brutality, even in this small area.

They were in every respect creating a mini-Afghanistan in this area of northeastern Iraq. Musab's people had acquired a quantity of ricin and other easily obtainable chemicals used for making dangerous chemical weapons and had begun experimenting on stray dogs.

Two years later, Zarqawi would finally pledge allegiance to bin Laden and proclaim himself the leader of a group called Tanzim Qaidat al-Jihad, the group that eventually became known as Al Qaeda in Iraq, then ISIS (Islamic State in Iraq). It is important to understand the following events that unfolded in these early years and literally "hurled" the heretofore unknown jihadi leader Zarqawi into international "jihadist/terrorist" fame.

FROM A JACK TO A KING IN TEN MINUTES: WITH A LITTLE HELP FROM AMERICA

As mentioned before, Zarqawi, soon after America's invasion of Afghanistan, had seemingly intuitively determined that America would be in Iraq within weeks. His men no doubt saw in him a great visionary having concluded such, and though he was likely smarter than average in these areas, in fairness, it should be pointed out that President George Bush had been signaling his intentions to pursue Saddam Hussain, for weeks. Iraq, under the leadership of Hussain, had been pointed out as a central point in President Bush's "Axis of Evil," along with Iran and North Korea. For anyone paying the slightest bit of attention however, it was obvious that his principal focus was Iraq, and more precisely Saddam.

Many saw this as somewhat of an obsession, chalking it up to Bush, the younger, intensely wishing to right a wrong attributed to his father, former president George Bush, the senior. The first President Bush had been sorely criticized for allowing the Iraqi army to escape back into their country following Desert Storm. President Bush Jr, many felt, was intent on avenging his father's honor.

Convincing congress and the American people to support an invasion of Iraq, especially while American troops were engaged in Afghanistan, wasn't as difficult as it may have seemed.

America was still reeling from the attacks of 9/11, and a sense of nationalism and unity against Islamic fundamentalism in general was thick in the air. Members of Congress sensed this national fervor and, as politicians, were eager to capitalize on it (it is instructive to see in this new century, the year 2020, and an election year, how so many who had supported the war currently try to rationalize their ill-advised decision). Few would object to such an invasion, but they needed a little more concrete intelligence to support it; thus, the "weapons of mass destruction" and to a lesser extent, an alliance between Iraq's Saddam Husain and Al Qaeda. In order to supply this final nudge into acquiescence, President Bush sorely needed compelling intelligence. It is worth noting here that "compelling" is a highly relative term. Still the Bush administration set about digging to get the supporting data, and they needed it soon, before the "post 9/11" nationalistic fervor subsided.

In fairness, President Bush was convinced of the necessity of the invasion of Iraq (later to be known as Operation Iraqi Freedom, "OIF," as opposed to the war in Afghanistan, Operation Enduring Freedom, "OEF"), but although convincing most in Congress wasn't going to be a big problem for him, he and his administration wanted to "seal the deal" in terms of supporting intelligence. In further "fairness to President Bush," regardless of how many politicians who choose to caveat their decisions in 2003, virtually all members of Congress supported OIF.

Their support was obtained in part by the supposition of Saddam's possession of weapons of mass destruction (WMD), though that, in later years, proved to have been a false supposition.

The greater impetus however was the claim at the time of Iraq's, and more importantly, Saddam's support of, and relationship with, Al Qaeda.

America had CIA intelligence operatives on the ground in northern Iraq, looking for just that.[2] The operatives were working in that "no man's land" region in the north, known to be the operations area for countless jihadi groups, especially in the short aftermath of America's invasion of Afghanistan. If there was to be proof of an Iraqi/Al Qaeda connection, it would be found here.

Though they kept an open mind and were diligently searching for that nexus, they found just the opposite. There was not only no evidence of a connection, but myriad evidence of a hatred for, and in some cases "fear of," Al Qaeda, on the part of Saddam's forces.

While American CIA operatives lurked in the shadows, virtually a stone's throw from jihadist operations areas, observing the movement and day-to-day activities of groups like Ansar al Islam and others, they could also, from their vantage point, watch Saddam's operatives lurking in similar shadows attempting to do the same thing. There was not only no visible connection but a much more visible disconnect between them and Al Qaeda. In short, they were much more akin to enemies than allies. There was no support for Al Qaeda in Iraq, and the operatives knew this and reported this. "This," however, was not what the Bush administration wanted to hear. Finally, an obscure report from the CIA operatives and analysts on the ground in northern Iraq changed everything. This simple, possibly one or two-line notation was/is synonymous with the "shot heard round the world," and at its core was the uneducated, former Jordanian delinquent/turned Islamic fundamentalist, *Ahmad Fadil Nazal al-Khalayleh*, now known as Abu Musab al-Zarqawi. The one, obscure, actually ironic connection between Iraq and Al Qaeda popped up in an intelligence report indicating that this unknown jihadist in the sea of unknown jihadists is identifying himself as "associated with Al Qaeda." Approximately minutes into his famous speech in February of 2003, in an attempt to establish a firm link between Iraqi President Saddam Hussain's government and Al Qaeda, behind General Colin Powell, on the wall, an ominous picture of Abu Musab al Zarqawi suddenly appeared, accompanied by the announcement from General Powell, that it was proof of the connection. In following years, General Powell would offer often heartfelt, though sometimes vague, apologies, though he has never actually admitted that he knew at the time it was a vast subterfuge. In fairness, he may not have known. In opposing fairness, however, it is highly unlikely.

Bush administration officials had been advised on several occasions by the intelligence operatives on the ground in northern Iraq that there was no evidence of any link between Iraq and Al Qaeda, and as a matter of fact, there was much more evidence of animosity and in some cases hatred between these two groups. The Bush folks now had the "contradictory" message they wanted to hear. Most analysts in hindsight (including the authors of this text) accept that the Bush administration knew that the Zarqawi connection was a weak one, and at worst, a subterfuge in order to accomplish an objective. Many (again, including the authors of this text) would later argue that the invasion of Iraq has contributed greatly to the American military's failure to secure Afghanistan to a level, allowing a complete withdrawal.

That said, Musab Zarqawi had pledged allegiance to Osama bin Laden, and he was in fact at the time in northern Iraq and considered to be something of a leader, though extremely minor. On balance however, it is unlikely at this time that Osama bin Laden knew he was there, and it is extremely unlikely that Saddam Hussain knew who he was, or that he was there in Iraq.

The intelligence operatives on several occasions even reported that the other jihadists operating in the area likely didn't know who Zarqawi was and almost certainly didn't care. Though the basic facts in General Powell's presentation were valid, the inference definitely was not. Who knew it at the time is speculative, but those who study these events should be aware of their foundations.

As for Zarqawi, it is also likely that he was both shocked and elated when he heard the news and saw his face beamed out to the entire world, describing him as just what he had for years wanted to be. Not yet 36 years old, he had been both ordained and crowned: ordained an international terror leader, on par with Osama bin Laden, and crowned as a brilliant terrorist strategist, by none other than the chief military officer of the most powerful country in the world, no doubt at the direction of the President of that country.

The confusion among bin Laden's top advisors and staff must have been palpable and chaotic. There's a slight chance bin Laden knew who he (Zarqawi) was, but there is a greater chance that he immediately scrambled his men to find out. Zarqawi had proudly introduced himself, for the past few years as tantamount to, the "right-hand man" to Al Qaeda leader Osama bin Laden. Now, America, the most powerful, influential country in the world was endorsing that claim. One thing was clear; bin Laden and Zarqawi would soon be tied at the hip for better or worse, often for better and worse simultaneously, alternating back and forth, often on a daily basis.

The Mukabarat (Jordan's anti-terror forces) operatives who had been pestered and burdened by Zarqawi since his days as a young delinquent and had by that time likely dismissed him, assuming he had actually become a bee farmer, or had been killed, were furious. In one fell swoop, this insignificant wannabe terrorist had been propelled to the status of rock star in the jihadi world.

"How the Hell could this have happened? This is bullshit," Abu Hatham, the top Mukabarat counterterror investigator and principal interrogator of Zarqawi, throughout his decades-long career as a petty crook-turned terrorist wannabe, is said to have screamed at the top of his lungs as he watched the speech on television.[3] His greatest fear and trepidation at that point lay in the fact that he also knew how ruthless and brutal Zarqawi could, and probably would be, as a result.

Abu Musab Zarqawi saw the moment as his "coming out" event and considered it a green light and probably an obligation to go about wreaking havoc on the world in the name of Allah, an obligation he accepted with relish. As soon as his friends back home, those he had tried unsuccessfully to recruit to join him in Afghanistan, stopped laughing uproariously, they probably glanced furtively at each other with a knowing wink, and rushed to be the first to travel to northern Iraq to join him. As a matter of fact, the level of commitment by the younger Islamic generation, the world over, increased precipitously that following year, and as jihadi recruits from all over the Islamic world poured into Iraq, the Bush administration's frantic search for an Al Qaeda–Iraq connection had finally borne fruit. It is likely that they saw themselves immediately as the "dog who had finally caught the car he'd been chasing and was unclear as to what to do with it."

TIME NOW, TO GET TO WORK

NOTE: *The next few sections of the text are going to be devoted to the birth and rise of the Islamic State, ISIS, IS, ISIL and Daesh, all common names for the single organization that originated from Al Qaeda in Iraq, headed by Abu Musab al-Zarqawi. We will refer to the group as ISIS. Other than the original Al Qaeda international terror organization, led by Osama bin Laden, ISIS*

131

has spawned more offshoot terror groups and attracted more volunteers to Islamic terrorism than any other. Thus, it is important for the student of this subject to understand as much as possible the people and the events involved, as well as the stages of development of ISIS. In short, a visual depiction of what would follow could very easily depict all the terror groups in the world in a pyramid with ISIS at the apex.

The announcement that one of Al Qaeda's top leaders was being given safe haven in northern Iraq worked for President Bush. Two thirds of the House of Representatives as well as the Senate approved and supported the use of military force in Iraq, a vote most of the still sitting members of Congress have been trying to disavow and/or find excuses for, to this day. It must be said that President Bush was not the first American President, democrat or republican, to twist the facts or use subterfuge to gain such authorization over the years. For Zarqawi, however, it was time to live up to the hype, which he did, reportedly, with zeal.

Zarqawi had two objectives in mind. Objective one was Jordan. He still hated the Jordanian royal family and wanted desperately to bring them down. He convinced himself that his was a "mission from God," as the Jordanian King was an apostate, deserving of death, but he was also still stinging from his treatment and imprisonment a few short years before. He couldn't wait to get revenge and to bring Jordan to its "spiritual" knees, metaphorically purifying it before Allah, and being responsible for forcing his country to return to the "pure" Islam of the Rashidun (rightly guided ones).

Author's Note: This is a good point for the student using this text to exercise a little psychological logic and draw some conclusions for yourself, like the authors have urged from the beginning. Assume the place and persona of Zarqawi using all the facts you've been given and try to "see through his eyes and feel what he's feeling." Remember, he began basically as a social failure and delinquent then through a religious conversion took on a personal mission that he saw as "Allah-inspired." Suddenly, all the hopes and desires he has harbored are within his reach, and nothing and no one, as far as he can tell, is going to be standing in his way. How would you respond, assuming that you have the same objectives. In reality and based on documented hindsight, Zarqawi is about to wreak havoc on that part of the world. The irony however is that he will (from his standpoint) use a fairly sophisticated form of strategy and as such will be successful for a very long period of time.

To do this, he was perfectly willing to kill every man, woman and child, in Jordan, in the name of Allah. After all, if they died, it was God's will, and they would have died a *Shahid* (martyr) immediately earning a place in paradise. His most impacting operation to the end of objective one came less than two years later.[1] He had his commanders plan to execute, on November 9, 2005, a series of suicide bombings at Amman, Jordan, high-end hotels around the city, locations he determined were sinful and westernized. One of these was at the Radisson Hotel in the lobby intentionally, targeting a wedding ceremony.

For this attack, his operations' planners had chosen a man and woman, newlyweds, traveling to Jordan, ostensibly to seek treatment for infertility (ironically, Zarqawi, in his religious zeal and piety, demanded that the two be legally married before being sent on this mission). The pair entered the lobby, bombs strapped to their bodies under their clothing, pretending to be casual observers, desirous of learning how such a wedding celebration is carried out. The man, Hussain Shamari, circled the outside of the crowded ballroom, filled with men, women and children, wearing their finest attire, happily dancing and celebrating this union, until he came to the head table where the father of the bride sat next to the father of the groom. He turned momentarily searching for his accomplice, Sajida Rashawi, but couldn't find her. He likely thought she had circled the opposite direction and was in place at the rear of the crowd, close to the entrance. He reached under his clothing and flipped the toggle switch that sent him, both fathers as well as more than 60 wedding guests to their deaths, wounding an additional 115 innocent souls.[1]

Sajida Rashawi watched from the rear of the ballroom. She had approached Zarqawi's people and volunteered and had been selected, in part, because she was slightly mentally impaired. She had recently lost her brother to an American assault in Iraq and sought revenge. Without detonating her bomb, she turned and walked away in shock, wandering the streets in her blood-spattered clothing, the bomb still strapped to her, until she was apprehended hours later.

Aside from carnage in Jordan, Zarqawi's other objective was to instigate a civil war between Sunni and Shiite and keep the war going as long as possible. As mentioned earlier, Zarqawi was, ironically, an adept strategist. He knew that he would be much more successful in his own war against America, in Iraq, if they had to expend valuable resources and time, quelling a civil war between the Iraqi Sunni and Iraqi Shiite.

America had unwittingly stoked a great deal of animosity between these two groups by removing all of Saddam Hussain's former Sunni military commanders (many of whom could have been of use to the west if they had been allowed to play a role) and replacing them with Shiite soldiers and commanders. All Zarqawi had to do was kill a few Shiite leaders, including highly revered Shiite clergy (whom he hated with a passion anyhow), in a manner in which the Sunni would be blamed, then sit back and watch as the "natural" occurred.

Whenever it seemed there'd be a lull in the fighting, or that there was a possibility the two sides may reconcile in some way, he'd simply order more suicide attacks against one side or the other, assuring the opposite side would be blamed. Soon, the "civil war," America feared, became the "insurgency" they feared even more.

For America, the worst thing that could happen in Iraq was a civil war and/or an insurgency (remember from this text, instruction on the nature and purpose of insurgencies). Success for America, even though President Bush declared it "accomplished," early in the operation, would never be achieved, as long as they had to play nanny to quarreling brothers.

Zarqawi met with immediate success in Iraq in part because the Sunnis of Iraq were supportive. He just set about "killing two birds." Following Saddam's capture and execution, America set up a governing council to help reorganize the Iraqi government and staffed it predominantly with Shiite. Zarqawi's simple task was convincing the nation's Sunni population that the intent was to give the country to the Shiite. From there, it took little encouragement for Zarqawi to elicit the Sunni's help in wiping out the Shiite whom, as stated earlier, he hated to begin with.

To give credit where credit is due, Zarqawi played this game from a strategic point, very masterfully. There was little concern on his part for, "collateral damage," so he wasn't hampered in this area. He followed the instructions of an instructional work titled, *The Management of Savagery*, which is still used by most terror leaders.[4,5]

In part, the man stresses extreme brutality as a "deity sanctioned" method of fighting a war, to the extent of using mentally disabled youth as suicide bombers as well as leaving young children in strategically placed, parked, explosive-laden vehicles so as not to draw suspicion until they could be detonated (children still inside). Such brutal tactics are commonplace among terror groups who don't shy away from such brutality as sending women and children out to accomplish operations, suicide vests strapped to their bodies, while their handler holds the detonator to ensure they don't get cold feet and fail to complete their mission.

They often drug these women and children in advance to ensure compliance.

Zarqawi, early in his campaign, launched a suicide bombing attack on the Jordanian embassy, again the "best of both worlds" as he still harbored a great deal of hatred for Jordan. The attack was seen as a Sunni attack directed toward harming the new "Shiite-led" government, which of course elicited a Shiite response.

Approximately one week later, he launched another suicide attack on the United Nations building in Baghdad, specifically targeting the much admired Argentinian UN Representative Sergio Vieira de Mello. De Mello was targeted additionally for his outspoken support for America and specifically President George Bush, with whom he had a close relationship. Again the Sunnis were blamed. Again the Shiite retaliated.[1]

In a more direct effort to pit the Shiite and Sunni communities against one another, he sent a suicide bomber (his own father-in-law, this time) to blow up one of the Shiite's most holy sites, the Imam Ali Mosque, but more specifically targeting the Shiite community's most revered holy figure, Ayatollah Mohammad Hakim. This attack too was successful, and by this time, Zarqawi had completed his task of miring the Sunni and Shiite in a civil war, one which the Americans would for years to come be required to spend valuable resources, time, and men, in trying to control.[1] This tactic also worked to drive the nation's Sunni closer to Zarqawi and his Sunni-populated ISIS. This was done in order to accomplish a common (to Zarqawi and the Sunni population as well) objective of destroying the now Shiite-controlled government.

For a relatively uneducated man, Zarqawi had proven himself to be a wise strategist and an enemy America would have to spend much time and resources to destroy.

NOTES

1 Weiss, M., & Hassan, H. (2015). *ISIS: Inside the army of terror*. London, UK: Phaidon Publishers.
2 Ghattas, K. (2020). *Black wave*. London, England: Headline Publishing Group.

3 Warrick, J. (2015). *Black flags: The rise of ISIS*. New York, NY: Doubleday.
4 Blumenthal, M. (n.d.). The management of savagery. *Verso*. Retrieved June 2, 2020, from https://www.versobooks.com/books/2868-the-management-of-savagery.
5 Naji, A. B., & McCants, W. (2006). The management of savagery: The most critical stage through which the Umma will pass. *Goodreads*. https://www.goodreads.com/book/show/25423277-the-management-of-savagery.

10

Birth of the Islamic State

At this point, Abu Musab al-Zarqawi was credited with the formation of Al Qaeda in Iraq (AQI) as well as ISIS. The Islamic State (as previously mentioned, they were/are often referred to as Daesh) was seen by many as a new mutation of an old demon, Abd al-Wahhab's Wahhabism, in its earliest and most extreme form. A natural progression for Zarqawi now was to declare the formation of the Islamic State, proclaiming himself the leader.

It is at this point and on this subject known that ISIS, Zarqawi and bin Laden were at greatest odds.[1] Bin Laden, throughout the Iraqi invasion and the operations carried out by Zarqawi (in the name of Al Qaeda, often much to the chagrin of bin Laden), most likely watched from somewhere in Pakistan. It is unclear whether he had settled in his compound in Abbottabad (the place he occupied when he was killed by US Navy SEALs) at that time, but it is virtually certain he was in Pakistan. It is also virtually certain that he was doing very little in terms of orchestrating operations of Al Qaeda, the organization he had birthed. Many believe that bin Laden, by his own choosing, was on the way out as leader of Al Qaeda. It is highly likely that Zarqawi's excessive televised brutality was the only thing keeping bin Laden involved, as he repeatedly chided the younger terror leader.

Zarqawi, on the other hand, alternated between claiming allegiance to and association with Al Qaeda, in his actions, and conducting operations as the leader of ISIS. It is also highly likely, and many analysts of the time attest to the fact, that bin Laden was often in a state of frustration and/or anger, at Zarqawi, while the younger terrorist leader seemed to almost enjoy pushing the limits just to increase bin Laden's frustration.

At times it seemed Zarqawi was almost saying, "you're old and out of the mainstream. I'm in charge now."

Osama bin Laden and Musab Zarqawi did share a desire to see the Islamic State brought back and recognized as legitimate, by the entire world.[2] The last formerly recognized Caliphate (Islamic State) had been disbanded by Turkey in 1924. A rebirth of the Islamic State, though not specified in the Quran or the Hadith, is widely accepted in the Islamic community around the world as a natural precursor to the return of the Mahdi, which in turn is a precursor to the end of time and dominance of the world by Islam.

Throughout history, there have been times when Islam was dominant in the world and the Caliphate or Islamic State reigned. Since the last Caliph reigned in Turkey, the desire for its resurgence has been strong, especially among fundamentalists such as the Wahhabists. Bin Laden and Zarqawi both saw this as a desired end state, an objective they both pursued. The only difference between the two terror leaders was how to achieve this.

Osama bin Laden saw the process as one in pursuit of a worldwide Islamic consensus involving all Muslims, including Shiite. As such, he determined that it would be done, but it would take time and would involve cajoling and coalition building. Zarqawi, on the other hand, as is the hubris of the young, was impatient and cared little for consensus building, and besides, he harbored a great hatred for many, the Shiite at the top of the list. As a matter of fact, most analysts believe Zarqawi's Islamic State probably didn't include the Shiite. After all, Zarqawi saw the Shiite, much like many Sunni do, as *kafir*, or the worst sort of unbelievers, legally subject to execution at the hand of the true believers.

Zarqawi's intent was to force the Islamic State on all Muslims with him as its leader. Those who did not comply and accept (including acceptance of his form of fundamentalism which seriously strangled and limited the freedoms and daily lives of moderate Muslims) would simply be done away with. Bin Laden, on the other hand, had a much more inclusive view, and while he like most Sunni was not enamored with the Shiite (in actuality, his mother was a Syrian Alawite, Shiite), he was pragmatic and knew that if a lasting caliphate was to form it would have to have the support of all Muslims, Sunni and Shiite alike. This disagreement between the two men served as the foundation for a myriad of periods of "falling out" to come. If Zarqawi had not been so elevated and "ordained" by General Colin Powell, most analysts agree bin Laden would likely have had him killed.

At any rate, the Islamic State was formed and Musab Zarqawi was unanimously accepted as its leader.

MIRED

Musab Zarqawi was virtually perfect for this time and place, in terms of establishing a recognizable Islamic State. He had a modicum of common sense in terms of strategy, and since Iraq very quickly became ruled by chaos and confusion, a "modicum" was all that was necessary, and he had been unwittingly endorsed by America's most powerful military commander, General Colin Powell.

Zarqawi, in addition to having a plan, hated everyone and therefore was capable of killing with little to no forethought. His hatred for the Shiite was well known and almost a prerequisite for Sunni in that area, but he had little respect for or concern for most of the Sunni Iraqi in the area as well. He considered the Iraqi Sunni as "a bunch of cowards who had little appetite for shahid."[3] He had no problem killing them when it was necessary.

He communicated with bin Laden during this time offering to swear "undying allegiance" to him and Al Qaeda, if bin Laden would get on board with his (Zarqawi's) plan of action, which basically consisted of killing anyone who didn't sign on to his "plan of action," until there was no one left but those who supported his Islamic State, with him as the leader. Bin Laden was no angel, but his strategy was a long term one that consisted of winning the "hearts and minds" of all Muslims, Sunni and Shiite alike. He had serious issues with Zarqawi's indiscriminate killing of other Muslims.

Bin Laden, himself, had been the object of an attempted suicide attack some years earlier. A group of serious fundamentalists in Saudi had determined that bin Laden was not "brutal" enough and launched an attack on a mosque where bin Laden was supposed to be worshiping one Friday.[4] As fate would have it, bin laden was not there that day. It is possible that this incident, which basically put bin Laden on the receiving end of such hatred and violence, may have to an extent ameliorated his future perceptions. Either way, he wasn't about to endorse Zarqawi's plans, but he also didn't want to alienate him for the time. He stalled, and it worked for a while.

For Zarqawi, bin Laden's support would have been nice, but he saw himself as being more in control than bin Laden at the time, a view shared by much of the world's intelligence agencies. The only issue with his line of thought was that Al Qaeda was and still is much more internationally grounded, while Zarqawi was, in spite of the attention drawn to him by General Powell, still a big fish (and at the time, getting larger by the day) in a small pond, Iraq. That said, America had to deal with him if there would be any hope of a stabilized Iraq. Bin Laden in the meantime simply said, if only metaphorically, "let me think about it."

Operation Iraqi Freedom became more and more confusing and chaotic, and the United States became more and more mired down in Iraq. To this day, there are still American troops in that country and real substantial stability is little more than a distant dream. At the time however, Zarqawi was pretty much directing the chaos and confusion, pitting virtually every militant group in the area, Sunni and Shiite alike, against each other, when and where it suited his plans.

He was playing the Iraqi theater like a composer conducts an orchestra. He had to be eliminated.

General Stanley McChrystal was in command of Task Force (TF) 626, made up of Army Delta operators, Special Forces, US Navy SEALs, Army Rangers and elements of the 160th Special Operations Aviation Regiment. The TF also included British Special Air Service and paratroopers. All these and more were assembled under the command of General McChrystal for one purpose, to hunt down and kill/capture Abu Musab al-Zarqawi.

The TF was successful in taking out Zarqawi on June 7, 2006, by airstrike, three years after General McChrystal took command, but not before he (Zarqawi) had successfully established the Islamic State (ISIS), which is still today in 2020, to varying degrees, depending on who you ask, operational.

The actual "takedown" of Zarqawi itself was not without mishaps, though General McChrystal and his special operators adjusted to these mishaps. Through an informant, the identity and location of Zarqawi's ubiquitous "Islamic spiritual advisor" were uncovered. The task force, using aerial capabilities, simply followed the young Islamic cleric for several days until he surreptitiously journeyed to a remote location, southeast of Baghdad in the country. The TF analysts watched the screen feed from the aerial platforms as the man made several clandestine movements, changing vehicles and directions at certain locations, and then finally arriving at a secluded house in the countryside.[2] As if on cue, a stocky man easily identified as Zarqawi came out of the house and greeted the cleric.

General McChrystal ordered two Delta Force teams on standby to board their helicopter gunships.

The teams, by operational doctrine, required two delivery helicopters for the operation. Ironically, one of the ships had mechanical problems and couldn't get airborne. Fortunately however, one of the F16 fighters, always on standby for the operation, was close by.

As Zarqawi and his mentor reentered the house, the General gave the go-ahead and the F16 released two smart bombs, completely destroying the structure. Zarqawi was alive when Delta operators arrived on scene by vehicle, but died within minutes. The last face he gazed into was an American Special Operations soldier. He was positively identified in part by the scar on his arm where he had cut away an offending tattoo, so many years before, while in prison.

THE ISLAMIC STATE (ISIS)

Abu Musab al-Zarqawi was dead, but his life of cruelty and penchant for hatred and brutality had spawned an entity that haunts the free world today. The Islamic State was and still is a vehicle for the most vicious of Islamic extremism. Its philosophy has engulfed young men and women from all parts of the globe, enticing them to commit the vilest of acts against their fellow man.

Countless lives have been ruined or lost as a result of the actions of this one man.

In the "tortoise and hare" race toward Islamic extremist domination of the world, it is safe to say that Al Qaeda had shown itself to be the tortoise during this time. Zarqawi had established the Islamic State from his formal organization of Al Qaeda in Iraq (later to be referred to as AQI by members of intelligence community) just by saying it was so, but he, throughout this period, had still courted Osama bin Laden, offering to swear allegiance to him in return for bin Laden's backing of his cruel agenda.

For his part, bin Laden was still stalling, possibly wanting to have his cake and eat it too. He knew Zarqawi, though cruel and barbaric, was attracting the attention of the entire world, and to an emerging power (emerging through the use of terror tactics, but emerging nonetheless) attention from the rest of the world is vital. Zarqawi had successfully established the Islamic State, but not the "Caliphate."

While some would say they are one and the same, and because there is no real Islamic governing body worldwide to define these things, so that there's really no "right or wrong" on the subject, the fact is, the term "Caliphate" carries weight that the term "Islamic State" does not. One (the former) is much more legitimate than the other.

Author's Note: From the perspective of the authors of this text, and based on hours of personal interviews with individuals, currently and formerly operational with ISIS, it is believed that many prominent members of the Islamic community around the world, perhaps through the Muslim Brotherhood or just as religious practitioners, do not formerly promote or reject the operations of such individuals as the late Musab Zarqawi for self-serving reasons of their own. This can easily be explained in part when you consider that their (the Zarqawi-like terror operators) actions allow to an extent an atmosphere in which the "moderates" can benefit by moving closer to their goals and objectives, while still allowing them political coverage in the sense that they are not vocally endorsing but still not vocally criticizing or condemning such actions. The terrorist activities of a few can benefit those moderates to some extent so they avoid "getting their hands dirty," but very definitely "partake of the resulting cake." For this reason, Muslim reformist like Dr. Zuhdi Jasser, founder and President of the American Islamic Forum for Democracy, and others strive to consistently pin down Muslim leaders around the globe on their positions relative to terrorism and extremism. Students of counterterrorism studies need to be aware of the possibility of such motivations.

Students of International Terrorism based on Islamic extremism have a tendency to try to understand Islam through the same parameters and through the same lenses they've used to understand their own religion, such as Catholicism or Protestantism. Such a practice leads to much confusion and misunderstanding.

In fairness, the authors of this text are neither Muslims nor experts in Islam. Having both taught and written on the subject of Islamic extremism for many years however, they are both experts on the misguided perceptions many lay persons and students bring to the subject. And in fairness, they are much more knowledgeable on the subject than most. As such, the following is an effort to lay a new foundation for understanding for students using this text.

There is not a "Vatican," or "Southern Baptist Association," type organization in Islam. There are some formal definitions of the term or concept, "Islamic State," as example, but even these definitions are widely disputed. "Islamic State," to some, is tantamount to Caliphate. Still, to others, the two could not be further from each other. The lack of a formal, universally agreed-upon definition of entities such as this has led to much confusion throughout history as well as the emergence of a multitude of Caliphs and "12th Imams" (many believe, the equivalent of Jesus among Shiite Muslims).

Therefore, when Musab Zarqawi declared the emergence of ISIS (Islamic State), with himself as the leader in 2004, and Abu Bakr al-Baghdadi, sometime after the death of Musab Zarqawi, declared himself the new leader of Islamic State and as such the Caliph, years later in 2014, it's hard to determine which organization was claiming supreme authority in Islam. To make matters more difficult, Al Qaeda, the most well-known Islamic extremist terror group in the world, was a little fuzzy on its own relationship with either of these men or their organizations. It is probably best not to try to "pigeon-hole" these groups or their roles in Islam. For some measure however, and much more formally, the last universally accepted Caliph and Caliphate were dismantled and declared null and void, by the Turkish government in 1924. For our purposes, Musab Zarqawi began the resurgence of an organized Islamic state, as described in the beginning of this text (Figure 10.1).

Zarqawi's Islamic State was built on a foundation of extreme cruelty and brutality. The guiding principle for it was forced acceptance and compliance. When Zarqawi was killed in 2006, his successor was selected in large part on his willingness and ability to continue that legacy.

The leader of the Islamic State, to replace Zarqawi, was chosen in much the same way that leaders of Islamic organizations and tribal groups have been selected throughout history, by the "Shura council" method.

The word "Shura" loosely translates to "consultation." As far back as the days of the Prophet Mohammad, Shuras were used to debate and to council leaders on appropriate decisions. They are, as one may expect, primarily made up of males and normally the eldest members of a group. A Shura is not unlike a "think tank" or a committee, and is no better or worse than any such organization, in terms of the appropriateness of decisions made. Such a group was used to select Zarqawi's successor, as leader of the Islamic State, just as a similar group was used to select the successor of the Prophet Mohammad.

Figure 10.1 A mugshot photo of Baghdadi detained at Camp Bucca, Iraq, in 2004.

It is important to keep in mind here that those involved in the Islamic State and the associated Shuras were confident that they were making decisions for the actual, prophetically foretold, emerging Islamic Caliphate (even though they didn't refer to the Islamic State as such at that time), the premier, all-powerful Islamic organization. The decisions as to the selection of successive leaders were not made quickly. Zarqawi's first successor, Abu Umar al-Baghdadi (note for the student: this is confusing and should be examined in order to keep it straight. The first leader of ISIS following Zarqawi's death was Abu *Umar* al-Baghdadi. His successor, following his death at the hands of American forces, and the more notable leader was Abu *Bakr* al-Baghdadi, who was also killed by American forces on October 27, 2019) was selected and appointed fairly

144

quickly, in 2006, but the organization was leaderless for a time while Umar's successor was named, after he was killed in a Special Operations raid in 2010.

The first time Abu Bakr al-Baghdadi (successor to Abu Umar al-Baghdadi) was officially heard from was in May 2011, when he delivered an eulogy for Osama bin Laden, following bin Laden's death at the hands of US Navy SEALs. Bakr al-Baghdadi was said to have been a descendent of the Prophet Mohammad (a requirement for the Caliph, it may be noted). Shortly after the American invasion of Iraq, when Zarqawi was beginning to organize the actual workings of Islamic State, Bakr was in the area organizing resistance groups. He was arrested in 2004 and held prisoner at Camp Bucca for a short time.

Bucca, an American-run prisoner-holding facility, was a poorly run prison where Iraqis suspected of subversive activities were held until American forces could figure out what to do with them. Some of the most extreme types, if the situation warranted it, were sent on to Guantanamo prison in Cuba where many still remain, but most were released from Bucca back into the area, once they were interrogated, and it had been determined to the extent, such could be determined, that they posed minimal or no threat to the Operation Iraqi Freedom mission and/or American forces. This was the most damaging of the "poorly conceived and administered" aspects of the prison process, and the release of Bakr al-Baghdadi was the most damaging decision made by Bucca officials in hindsight.

Bucca, like many holding areas there and in Afghanistan, was a perfect place for insurgents and subversives to meet, network and hone their re-sistance skills. Baghdadi came out of his short term of confinement to be a much smarter and more well-connected organizer of jihadis. Those con-fined at Bucca would routinely write their network and contacts' phone numbers and contact information on the linings of their underwear where such was usually safe from detection by Bucca officials.

Bakr al-Baghdadi soon came to the notice of the top members of the Islamic State operational administrators and Shura council members. Who he was and the reputation he was building were becoming known to the Shura when Zarqawi was killed and throughout the relatively short period of time ISIS was headed by his predecessor, Umar Baghdadi. He was at the right place, at the right time, and was seen as a good fit to replace Umar.

Bakr al-Baghdadi was smart. His persona was completely opposite of the brashness and ostentatiousness of Zarqawi though, he proved himself soon enough to be just as brutal. His succession to the leadership was announced in the appropriate circles, but he himself kept fairly quiet (save for eulogizing bin Laden in 2011) until he came out "with a bang" in 2014. On that day, he introduced himself to the world, not as the leader of Islamic State, but as the "Caliph" himself, and proclaimed that there was no Syria, no Iraq, only the lands of the Fertile Crescent, over which he reigned. There were further only two categories of human beings: those who supported the Caliphate and him, and those who were infidels, deserving of death. For the layperson, such was tantamount to announcing that he was the returning Jesus the Savior, and the kingdom he headed was the new "Heaven on Earth."[5]

(For the student, this is a good time to update your timeline, using Al Qaeda, Islamic State comparisons.)

During this period, following the death of Osama bin Laden, his second-in-command Ayman al-Zawahiri, had taken the reins of Al Qaeda. Zawahiri was the individual most analysts believe orchestrated the killing of Abdullah Azam, bin Laden's associate in the early days of the Pakistan operation to assist the Afghan mujahideen in their war against Russia. To date, Zawahiri is still considered the leader of Al Qaeda, though to his extreme lack of charisma and failure to live up to the persona of bin Laden, many, including bin Laden's son Hamza bin Laden, have been considered as replacements (Hamza bin Laden was killed in US counterterrorism operation, September 14, 2019).

The relationship between Zawahiri and Bakr al-Baghdadi was much the same as the relationship between Zarqawi and bin Laden. At this time, and even still today, the Islamic State had succeeded in upstaging Al Qaeda as the top Islamic extremist terror organization in the world. More organizations around the globe were beginning to swear allegiance to ISIS than to Al Qaeda. The basic dynamics of the two groups were pretty much the same as well. ISIS was just as brutal (many believe much more so) and Al Qaeda was still struggling for relevance and though it obviously pained them, taking their cues from ISIS.

Zawahiri often condemned the brutality of ISIS and the wanton killing of other Muslims. Baghdadi was very definitely engaging in a form of Takfirism (an Islamic practice in which someone, in this case Baghdadi himself, has the power to identify those who are "Takfir," heathen unbelievers, and sentence them to death), his victims being overwhelmingly whole groups of other Muslims. Zawahiri condemned this behavior but only strong enough to get it on record and not strong enough to urge its cessation.

COMMAND AND CONTROL

In a very real sense, ISIS and Al Qaeda as well as the other international terror organizations are small, mostly ineffective (depending on how you measure effectiveness), armies. They have all the trappings of a highly organized national army and, in some ways, are operationally superior to the armies of many small, developing nations. These trappings and characteristics, some seemingly minor, are what makes an army effective and successful. One of these is a well-run system of Chain of Command and Command and Control (C&C).

We won't go into a lesson on these two areas here, but they are not as simple as they may seem. In a nutshell, a good system of C&C assures people at the top know what people at the bottom are doing, and can encourage its continuance or cessation. ISIS, and even Al Qaeda in its prime, never had these systems functioning the way they should have for maximum efficiency. As a result, on a smaller scale, ISIS local commanders were killing, looting and exercising extreme unnecessary control over smaller locales, alienating the populations at a time when those at the top were trying to unify Muslims under one banner and for a single purpose. This very fact prevented ISIS and Al Qaeda from ever having an effective relationship, much to the relief of those of us who were combating them.

There were several reasons for this lack of control, but the major cause was a highly ineffective method of selection of top leaders. A bunch of "good old boys" who came together and formed the Shuras charged with selection of successive leaders for the Islamic State were pretty much doomed to failure. The idea of "God's will" guiding their hand may not have been detrimental in and of itself, but when it was the only guiding criteria, which it often was, success in this area was highly elusive while failure was a foregone conclusion.

The leadership successions early on adopted a process following the actual selection of a leader that initially assures the religious credentials satisfying the "Allah's will" caveat, of the chosen, very early in the process. As with all other activities of these groups, it is imperative that not only their members, but the rest of the world, be comfortable that

147

everything they do, no matter how horrific, is blessed, and this begins with the bonafides of the chosen leaders.

This validation process is followed by a lengthy period (as long as feasible under the circumstances) during which the actual identity of the successor is protected. Therefore, those in charge of the process can announce, "we have the most perfectly, Godly anointed leader selected," and as long as no one knows who they are, they can't dispute this assertion. This is continued along enough, hopefully for this part of the bonafides of the leader to become a foregone conclusion, much like an afterthought. This also allows for a period of time for the past leaders to ascend into a type of historic martyrdom, again subliminally.

Abu Umar al-Baghdadi, the initial successor to Zarqawi, was selected, in addition to the "God's will" criteria, because of a "scholarly aptitude," a veteran of combat, and the assumption that he had some claim to the bloodline of the Prophet Mohammad. Each of the first three leaders of ISIS, as a matter of fact, claimed Quraysh tribal lineage which would give them a potential bloodline link to the Prophet Mohammad. Umar and his successors were awarded the title Amir al Mu'minin (Commander of the Faithful), a title that was also claimed by Mullah Mohammad Omar, the founder and commander of Afghanistan's Taliban. The fact that there were many "Amir al Mu'minin's" running around was not a problem since the "faithful" they commanded referred to the group of "faithful" that specifically followed them.

The principal problem with Umar was that he had little control and no semblance of command, based on control. He was, for the most part, unaware of what his people on the ground at the local level were doing in the name of the Islamic State. In hindsight, he may not have even understood that he should have such control, having no concept of anything approximating C&C. He would occasionally be told by people who were trying to be faithful to the Caliphate that his men in some villages were looting and raping, and his response would generally be, "Yes, I'm aware of that. I ordered them to do it."

Now, desiring the support of the local populace is generally a political consideration, and terrorism, rooted in Islam (since Islamic extremism-fueled terrorism has a purely religious objective), has ironically had little concern for politics, since, and except for, the birth of Wahhabism. The issue here however is if the Islamic State was ever going to be viable and continue to survive and grow, the way they intended, the support of the public was vital. As stated, Umar was being told now and then that his men out in the villages were terrorizing, looting, murdering and raping in the name of "the purity of Islam as exhibited by this new Islamic State," but he either didn't believe it or didn't know what to do about it, and usually responded with, "yes I'm aware of it." This soon turned out to be a moot point at any rate since Umar was killed by American special operators in 2010.

Like Abu Umar, Abu Bakr was fairly unknown when the shura selected him to replace Umar. He would soon, however, become known to most of the world, beginning with the July 2014 proclamation of the official Caliphate formation, with him as the Caliph. He did this at the Grand Mosque of al-Nuri in Baghdad, with its famous leaning minaret (the minaret is said to have "bowed to the Prophet Mohammad," as he passed overhead on his ascension to Heaven).

All of the leaders of these movements and terror groups have deployed some sort of strong symbolism when they announced themselves to the world. Mullah Omar, leader of the Taliban, actually donned a cloak kept in a mosque in Kandahar, said to have once been worn by the Prophet Mohammad.[6]

Such symbolism is extremely important to a movement such as ISIS since there is an intent to establish legitimacy and permanency. Not all terrorist organizations and movements wish to establish permanency, but ISIS, since it claims statehood, does. We will get back to Abu Bakr al-Baghdadi in a moment, but this distinction should be made at this point.

Early in this text we pointed out that terror groups all have one of two motives or ultimate objectives, and they are either political or religious. Some Islamic terror groups may be said to embrace both since religion and politics are so intertwined in Islam, but the immediate objective will be either religion-based or politically-based.

Al Qaeda for instance isn't intent on an immediate ISIS, as its objective is more of an intent to return all mankind to pure Islam, governed by *shariah*. The Islamic State however is just what it asserts, a state. As such the intent is for the world to recognize them as an official governing entity, complete with all the trappings, "infrastructure, governing boards, service provision to those governed, etc."

If you think about it, there is no formal way for an entity to be recognized as an official "state" or government. There are however four mostly acceptable steps to this end:

1. Eligibility (eligibility in this case is "in the eyes of the beholder")
2. Accepted independence (you have to overcome the claims of any other country over your sovereignty)

3. Recognition (the problem is, recognition by "whom")
4. Obtain final stamp of approval (again however, from whom)

This will come as no surprise, but Islamic terror groups don't usually proceed according to any acceptable set of rules. The Islamic State however does want to be recognized. They aren't particular about how this recognition is obtained, but they do want the world to see them as a state worthy of a seat at the United Nations. Now it's important here to realize that a religious-based entity such as ISIS first craves "recognition from their deity" or the blessings of Allah. As long as they have this, they can simply demand recognition from the rest of the world, and of course, all they need to have "this recognition" is their own assertion, which is what al-Baghdadi proclaimed from the podium at the al Nuri mosque in June of 2014.

The rest, he and the leaders of ISIS planned to take by force. Again, as has been stated in this text, this is the major difference between Osama bin Laden and the Al Qaeda philosophy, and, Al-Zarqawi, Umar Baghdadi and future leaders of ISIS. Bin laden wanted to "woo" the Islamic people and having accomplished that, the rest of the world, while ISIS leaders were content with killing all those who wouldn't go along. We will see these two ideologies clash from that time, through today, as we continue.

ABU BAKR AL-BAGHDADI

One of the dichotomies of cruel tyrannical leaders is that they maintain order. The order they maintain is of their own design and depiction, but it is "order" and few if any are willing to step out of line. There's a huge price to pay, but the order is palpable and highly visible. Mullah Omar's Taliban established order. Pol Pot established order in Cambodia. Of course he killed thousands in doing so, but the order was there. And in Iraq, Saddam Hussain had established and maintained order throughout the country for decades.

Once such a leader is deposed or killed, throughout the period of jubilation, there's a simmering ominous question in the minds of those celebrating the demise of cruelty: "what happens now." It usually doesn't take long for these same people (keep in mind that in nations like Iraq, jihadists and terrorists make up a minuscule percentage of the overall population. The rest of the people are highly similar to you and me, with families and jobs and familiar goals and objectives) to realize that the cherished order is no longer there, and it has been replaced by highly impacting confusion, chaos and bewilderment, and not a few, really bad guys who are bent on stealing, looting, murdering and settling old scores, outside the boundaries of the law. As is human nature, these same people soon forget the price they paid for the aforementioned order, and begin longing for it, maybe not the person who provided it, but definitely "it."

Members of the Bush administration made some really serious errors which exacerbated this chaos and confusion, namely Paul Bremer, President Bush's Provisional Authority head. Bremer appointed a highly partial group of Shiite leaders, with very little Sunni representation, to lead the country until a President could be elected, again contributing a great deal to the fear and confusion of the country's Sunni population. The fear was that America was intent on turning the nation into a Shiite nation, excluding anything, "Sunni." In such situations, jihadists can easily step in to save the day. Zarqawi, followed by Umar Baghdadi and then Abu Bakr al-Baghdadi, found themselves in a perfect situation. They definitely benefited from the adage "to be successful, find a need and fill it."

Following the death of Zarqawi and that of Umar Baghdadi, Abu Bakr al-Baghdadi was chosen to lead ISIS in 2010 and officially introduced himself to the world at his "coming out" party in 2014. He would remain in that leadership position until his death at the hands of US Army 75th Rangers and Delta Force operators in October 2019. Nine years under those conditions was considered a highly successful run.

The anti-American jihadi leader in Iraq following the removal and eventual execution of Saddam Hussain appeared rather spontaneously. Generally speaking, leaders in just about any culture or environment evolve slowly over a period of time, but the situation, as it were at this time and place, called for a different scenario.

Most of these "leaders" were up to the point of their appearance on the scene, unknown, and as in the case of Musab Zarqawi for instance, would probably never have appeared and gained prominence if not for incidents such as the unexpected exaltation of him by General Colin Powell. Ironically, he probably would have died on the vine had it not been for this.

Bakr al-Baghdadi's rise to prominence came in large part because of the method in which he and other detainees of America were handled. The prisons (or holding areas if you will, since most of these men were not convicted of any crimes, simply suspected of being enemies of the

Iraqi government), such as the detention facility at Camp Bucca, were very poorly organized. In their defense however, there was no time to establish more secure environments to hold and interrogate these individuals. All of these facilities were set up, virtually overnight. One of the most negatively impacting oversights in these environments was the lack of segregation operations. Detainees were held together and allowed every opportunity to congregate and communicate (America was then, and still is, very cognizant of the local culture, religion and social fabric, and concerned that they would overstep these lines). The problem is that this was a perfect breeding ground for networking and more so, for leaders to evolve.

Those with some education and insight into human behavior were extremely attractive to others, searching for leadership. They gravitated to them.

Virtually every individual in these holding areas was of the same mindset; they were victims of a severe injustice, based on their perceptions (remember perceptions are never right or wrong, they just "are"), and as far as they were concerned, they had every right to be incensed and to "fight back." All they needed was someone, around whom they could coalesce. Bakr al-Baghdadi was just such a person. He entered the facility, unknown, and in a very short period of time (he was released less than a year later), rose to the position of "leader," and was released, reputation intact and well known. More importantly, he himself saw this. Many say that his parting words to American forces upon his departure were, "I'll see you guys in New York." The problem for America was that he himself (Baghdadi) was convinced of his position. The only thing remaining at this point was for him to make himself available to lead ISIS. As far as he was concerned, his acceptance to this position was a foregone conclusion. We know how the rest of this story unfolded!

Once Baghdadi took control of ISIS (formerly Al Qaeda in Iraq, or "AQI", organized and run initially by Zarqawi), he easily stepped into the shoes of his predecessor and endeavored to amplify the brutality and atrocities foisted on the people, by Zarqawi. He orchestrated and in many cases took part in sexual slavery, rape, floggings and random executions of all who opposed or even questioned him, especially the Yazidis of Iraq.

Author's Note: Remember, these people were surrounded by people who were respected religious figures who were telling them that such behavior was not only Quaranically accepted, but even required by Allah. There were even a set of rules set

*forth by the religious advisors and based on their interpretation
of the Quran, which entailed which young females who were to
be kept as slaves and which were to be sexually exploited. Those
above the age of 12 were to be subjected to this behavior and
those younger were to be simply held until they reached the age.
Any basic human behavior issues or hesitations due to simple
common decency were expelled as a result of the local Mullah,
who was always on hand to (religiously) rubberstamp the
actions.*

Baghdadi seemed to take personal pleasure in the sexual domination of
his adversaries, even going so far as to keep several sex slaves for his
personal use, all the while preaching the religious sanctioning of his
actions. In 2013, an American humanitarian aid worker, Kayla Mueller,
was kidnapped by ISIS. Baghdadi held Mueller for years, and it is reported that she was tortured innumerable times and was forced to do his
sexual bidding.[7]

She is believed to have been killed by the hands of ISIS in 2015. ISIS
claims it was a Jordanian bomber that targeted the building where she
was held, responsible for her death. Her body has never been recovered.[8]
In October of 2019, the United States conducted "Operation Kayla
Mueller," the mission that ultimately led to the death of Baghdadi.

Remember, the importance of religiously validating their deeds
however evil was of utmost importance to this generation of jihadi terrorist. As for Baghdadi, he seemed at all times to be on a mission to show
the world that he could be more vicious and cruel than any who had
gone before him.

*Author's Note: Stepping out of the historic lane for a moment, it
is important for the student of these times and these people
(those who use violence and terrorism to achieve objectives) to
remember that when an individual gains such control and power
over their fellow man with little or no consequences, it is often
the case that the original political or religious objectives give
way to the sheer pleasure of the power they have. The idea that if
they so choose, they may take part in the ultimate display of
power, by ending the life of another human being, often in
gruesome ways, becomes intoxicating to the point that the original goal or objective is simply lost, replaced by pure joy. If you
consider additionally that most of these individuals are still*

153

young, and uninhibited, prone to act without concern for the effects of their actions, and that many have experienced or witnessed brutality, it is easy to see how such things can become commonplace. Young followers of Zarqawi and later Baghdadi frequently held auctions at which their sex slaves could be bought and sold, or simply traded them or gave them to others as "sex slave" gifts. Such practices are common, still today among these terror groups.

Abu Bakr al-Baghdadi, like most of the fundamentalist jihadists of the era, changed his name. He went through several iterations of alias', but the name he chose as caliph (Abu Bakr) almost certainly represented the first caliph following the death of the Prophet Mohammad, Abu Bakr.

The original Abu Bakr was, in addition to being the first successor of the Prophet, one of the four rashidun, or "rightly guided ones," referred to as such because of their personal relationship to the Prophet while he was still alive. These four (Abu Bakr, Umar, Uthman and Ali) are the most venerated Islamic leaders even today, and any generational or even incidental connection to any of them adds a great deal of respect to a contemporary Islamic leader.

Of course, as the self-proclaimed Caliph, even though much of his respect and control came as a result of violence and threat, Baghdadi still needed to augment his bonafides as much as possible. Very little was known about Baghdadi before he came to prominence as the caliph and leader of ISIS or ISIL (remember, Islamic State of Iraq and the Levant is an alternate title often used for ISIS). The Levant refers to an area that includes most of the Middle East.

Baghdadi was, according to most who knew him in his earlier life, "quiet and unassuming." This "ghostly past" (little is known about him as a result of his "quiet, unassuming" persona) served him well when he was put in the holding facility at Camp Bucca and came to be seen by his peers as having leadership qualities.

Human nature is such that the "unknowns" about a person in such a position usually generate more positive and powerful illusions; therefore, if a group see a person in a positive light and knows nothing about their past, they tend to assume that their past is powerful and positive for them. Unless more is actually known, a strong person is assumed to have been strong in their past, a decisive person is assumed to have always been decisive, etc. Baghdadi managed this "unknown" well and always used it to his advantage.

The only thing of note is that a younger Baghdadi, after the invasion of Iraq, by US forces, helped to form a minor militant group. It is unknown just how much influence he had in forming the group, but here again, that unknown morphed into a scenario in which he was much more in control of the group and possessing of much greater leadership qualities at that time. The group Jamaat al-Sunnah was merged into ISIS.[2]

Abu Bakr al-Baghdadi became much more vocal and active in ordering attacks, following the death of Osama bin Laden in 2011. Many analysts believe that he gained momentum as leader of the organization as a result of these retaliation attacks, claiming them as revenge for bin Laden's killing. He seemed to gain a lot of confidence during this period. The more accolades and praises he received, the more confident he became. Unfortunately, the American media is often culpable in aggrandizing those who should be condemned or ostracized by the civilized world. As detailed earlier in his text, for example, Musab Zarqawi benefited a great deal from this, once he was introduced to the world by the Bush administration and given an undeserved, lofty stature in the world of Islamic extremism and terrorism.

ISIS IN SYRIA: THE RIGHT PLACE AT THE RIGHT TIME

Sometime before 2013, Baghdadi sent a trusted compatriot and lower level ISIS commander, Abu Muhammad al-Julani, to Syria to organize an ISIS front in that country. The Syrian uprising that began in 2011 generated fertile ground for several Islamic fundamentalist groups to gain a foothold, due to the extreme chaos and confusion (a situation that still exists at the writing of this text), and Baghdadi wanted to make sure ISIS availed itself of this opportunity.

Author's Note: Terrorist organizations always flourish in areas that are plagued by confusion and chaos and a general lack of governance.

Baghdadi provided Julani with men and money, and as a result, in short order, the "Al-Nusra front (aka Jabhat al-Nusra)" was born in Syria, led by Julani. His (Baghdadi's) intent was to integrate his movement with the revolutionaries in Syria. Soon however, the relationship between the two leaders and these two groups began to break down.

155

Muhammad Julani (as of today, still commanding the al-Nusra front) proved to be as effective as Baghdadi, if not more so, as a leader and organizer, and soon al-Nusra became the most powerful rebel group in Syria. Julani and Baghdadi, however, were very different in terms of leadership styles and more importantly, the casual use of violence and brutality, which had come so easy to Baghdadi and Zarqawi before him.

Possibly because he saw the reluctance of Julani to exemplify his style, Baghdadi in late 2013 ordered Julani to dissolve al-Nusra as an independent organization and allow it to be absorbed into ISIS. It is also possible, and even highly likely, that Baghdadi had seen Julani becoming more respected and popular, precisely because he was unwilling to use the level of brutality, for which Baghdadi had become known.

Such tactics even when Zarqawi was alive and active had long been decried by bin Laden and by the Islamic community at large. Julani's less brutal methods were likely a relief to Muslims throughout the region and the fact that he had achieved a level of success that rivaled Baghdadi's was no doubt a source of extreme irritation to the ISIS leader. As for Baghdadi, he still considered Julani a subordinate and saw al-Nusra, a legitimate domain of ISIS, under his ultimate command. Julani saw things differently.

Though Julani had sworn al-Nusra's allegiance to Al Qaeda in Iraq (formally, through the ISIS chain of command), he now cut out the middleman and declared al-Nusra a direct and independent subordinate to Al Qaeda. In a sense, he ignored Baghdadi and subordinated himself and al-Nusra directly to Zawahiri and the umbrella Al Qaeda organization in Iraq.

Such a move gave Al Qaeda leadership the right to step in and supersede Baghdadi's wishes and command authority. In reality, they (AQI) already had this authority, and Julani's actions seemed to just throw this in Baghdadi's face. At the time this all occurred, which of course was following the death of bin Laden, Egyptian born Ayman al-Zawahiri, bin Laden's longtime compatriot, had assumed command of Al Qaeda (such is still the case at the writing of this text). Zawahiri was no doubt supportive of Julani's attempts since he was in line with the late bin Laden's thought processes, condemning the extreme brutality of first Zarqawi and then Baghdadi.

This situation was synonymous to a fight between sibling brothers, one of whom had been the older, more powerful of the two. Now as the father (Zawahiri) steps in, it is plain to see that he favors in more ways than one the younger (Julani). For multiple reasons, the two men were

156

inclined to accept the authority of Zawahiri, the leader of Al Qaeda, which was still considered the most powerful (especially when it came to funding) terror group in the world. At Zawahiri's direction, al-Nusra became Al Qaeda's direct subsidiary in Syria, basically bypassing ISIS and Baghdadi. Clashes between the two groups followed for a time, but the decision stood.

> *NOTE: It should be understood here that Zarqawi and later Baghdadi were allowed by Al Qaeda to continue their operations, even though their methods were extremely troubling, primarily because they achieved results. Bin Laden and now Zawahiri were accepting of the violence since it was effective (this theme has played out in far too many circles of influential Muslim leaders around the world, even today).*

Today, al-Nusra is a much more respected group in Syria than ISIS. The umbrella group most effective in opposing the dictator, Assad, the Free Syrian Army, works closely with al-Nusra and Jalani, but not as often with ISIS. Al-Nusra is made up of mostly Syrian fighters, while ISIS is populated by more foreign fighters, and the level of violence against non-combatants, while still at a high, with ISIS fighters, is seen only rarely with al-Nusra.

Another issue of importance in Syria is one that has been a problem for foreign fighters in many conflicts in the Middle East, including Iraq and Afghanistan, namely the imposition of the harshest of Islamic fundamentalism on people who, though religious, are not willing to give up their freedoms.

> *Author's Note: Keep in mind that the ultimate goal of these groups is recognition and permanence, a platform from which they can expand theoretically, into the entire world. This permanence and recognition, however, will mean nothing if the established government they seek isn't fundamentalist in nature and doesn't follow the strictest of shariah law. That's why they exist in the first place and to give this up in order to be recognized is tantamount to a Christian giving up belief in the resurrection, in order to be allowed to stay alive. It's just not going to happen. For this reason, from the very beginning of gaining control of a territory, this structure is put into place by the terrorist organization as if to say, "we're going to provide a*

functioning government for you but these are the rules you're going to live by so you may as well get used to it from the beginning." This same logic and supporting theory should be applied to the attempt at normalizing relations between the Afghan government and the Taliban. If the Taliban gain any legitimacy or control in that country, they will apply their brand of Islamism. That's the purpose for their existence, and they will never compromise on this.

This was an issue with the Arab fighters who came to Afghanistan to help the people rid themselves of the Russian invaders. It was an issue with the Taliban who organized and set forth in an effort to rid the countryside of criminals and robbers. It was an issue with Zarqawi and Al Qaeda in Iraq, and it was an issue with the successors of Zarqawi, namely Abu Bakr al-Baghdadi.

It is also an issue, by the way, with the African-based terror groups, Boko Haram and al-Shabob.

If analyzed, it is easy to understand why this issue is so prevalent. The objectives and goals of Islamic fundamentalist groups are "deity driven." They are, in effect, on a mission from God. Of course, there is ample room for this "deity driven," ostensibly pure objective to bring the people closer to God through the purest, most righteous of lives, can easily be bastardized and become something horrendous and cruel.[1] Throughout history, in every religion, those who have launched on a mission from God have often become tyrants who have done far more harm than good, but this is especially true for the Islamic fundamentalist. While at the foundation of Christianity, in terms of behavior, there is an admonition, "you shouldn't do *this* because God would be displeased," at the foundation of fundamental, Islam is the admonition, *"this,* is forbidden," and such proclamations are more often than not enforced by special, "morality police" units, even today and even in supposedly modern societies such as Saudi Arabia. The idea that the choice to do right as opposed to wrong is not available to the average citizen in many Islamic cultures and is not even "heard of" in cultures controlled by fundamentalists like Al Qaeda or ISIS is enforced by torture, public humiliation and often extremely harsh punishment.

Before American forces routed the Taliban in Afghanistan in early 2000, it was not unusual to see these "morality police" roaming the streets in Kabul or Mazer e-Sharif, beating men and women who were

158

not in strict compliance, and normally such compliance was in the eyes of the beholder, "beholder" in this case being the police themselves.

Virtually every area that has come under the control of fundamentals like Baghdadi or bin Laden or Zarqawi has suffered through such humiliation and control. In Syria however, Julani's al-Nusra front didn't do this. It may have been intentional or it could have been that he just "had bigger fish to fry," but the fact itself, along with the fact that the Nusra front was an aid to the Free Syria Army, allowed him to be more successful.

It also virtually assured that Al Qaeda leader Zawahiri would side with him in the disagreement between him and Baghdadi. In the aftermath, Baghdadi fumed a while, launched a few retaliatory strikes designed to punish Jalani and al-Nusra, and then soon let it go. Today, al-Nusra is considered more of an enemy toward Bashar al-Assad and the oppressive Syrian government than America and the west, and of course Bakr al-Baghdadi is dead.

As for Abu Bakr al-Baghdadi, in October 2019, facing imminent capture by US army 75th Rangers and Delta operatives, Baghdadi detonated a suicide vest, killing two children along with himself. His life ended much the same as he had lived for years. His demise is in its purest from a living example of the adage, "live by the sword." Additionally, his wanton disregard and slaughter of the innocent were played out to the end as if to signal to the world his intent to cling to the monster he was, even in death. One thing the world did see in his end is the basic cowardly instinct of so many of these terror leaders. Though this will never be known for sure, it is obvious that Baghdadi's clinging to the children in his final moments was a cowardly attempt at avoiding his own death.

NOTES

1 McCants, W. (2015). *The ISIS apocalypse: The history, strategy, and doomsday vision of the Islamic State*. New York, NY: St. Martins Press.
2 Warrick, J. (2015). *Black flags: The rise of ISIS*. New York, NY: Doubleday.
3 Weiss, M. & Hassan, H. (2015). *ISIS: Inside the army of terror*. London, England: Phaidon Publishers.
4 Trofimov, Y. (2008). *The siege of Mecca: The 1979 uprising at Islam's holiest shrine*. New York, NY: Anchor.
5 Sanders, L. (2019, October 27). Who was the 'Islamic State' leader Abu Bakr al-Baghdadi? *DW Akademie*.

6 Rashid, A. (2010). *Taliban*. New Haven, CT: Yale University Press.
7 Calamur, K. (2015, February 10). Family confirms U.S. hostage Kayla Mueller dead. *NPR*. Available from https://www.npr.org/sections/thetwo-way/2015/02/10/385182490/u-s-hostage-kayla-mueller-con firmed-dead.
8 https://www.nytimes.com/2015/02/11/world/middleeast/parents-of-kayla-mueller-isis-hostage-confirm-she-is-dead.

11

Women within Terrorism
New Tactics and What We Can Expect Next

WOMEN WITHIN TERRORISM: BY CHANCE AND BY CHOICE

The following sections in this text focus on women within terrorism and new terrorist threats and tactics. The reason these sections are included in this text is that, while we have devoted a considerable amount of time looking at the history of terrorists, we want to leave the reader with an understanding of terror threats today and those to come.

It is important to note that some of the women who've become members of ISIS voluntarily joined the terrorist group or acted on behalf of a terrorist group. This section will examine these individual women as well as women who've become embedded in terrorist organizations against their will. This topic is of particular interest today, in 2020, in light of the "me too" movement within the United States and the growing number of female leaders on the world stage.

In 2014, prior to the "me too" female empowerment movement in America, the world was shocked to learn that 276 schoolgirls had been kidnapped by Boko Haram in Chibok, Nigeria.

When this horrific event took place, Barack Obama was America's President. His wife, first lady Michelle Obama, gave considerable attention to the kidnapped schoolgirls, posing on social media with a sign that read "#BringBackOurGirls."[1]

Her attempt at gaining exposure of this horrific event proved fruitful to an extent, and many leaders throughout the world worked with Nigerian leaders to bring the girls home. This is an example of how the power of social media can reach a mass audience and advance a cause for good.

Social media is useful to counter terrorism, such as in the case of the Chibok girls, but has also proven effective for terrorist groups and their nefarious purposes (i.e., gaining sympathizers, recruiting, radicalizing and financing their groups).

Analyzing the kidnapping of the Chibok girls is fascinating in more ways than one. Many of these girls that were ripped from their families and forced to marry men twice their age, bear their children and become enslaved, eventually fell in love with these men, and, following their rescue, indicated a strong desire to return to their lives under Boko Haram rule.

This may be better understood when considering the fact that the schoolgirls that married men of status within Boko Haram suddenly discovered a life of "luxury" in which they had ample food, respect from the other girls as well as men within the terrorist group, and servants (other kidnapped girls) to do their bidding. Adherence to, or belief in, the Boko Haram ideology was of little importance to them as long as they were afforded those luxuries.

A victim identifying with, sympathizing or falling in love with their captor is not extremely rare (known as Stockholm Syndrome). There have been recorded accounts of such cases occurring throughout history. One particular example, gaining international notoriety at the time, was that of the kidnapping of heiress, Patty Hearst.

Hearst was kidnapped at the age of 19 by a radical organization known as The Symbionese Liberation Army (SLA). This group was a radical left-wing army that believed in equality for all races, genders and ethnicities and spoke out about a society based on peace and love. Ironically, their means of achieving this goal was kidnappings, murder and homemade crude bomb attacks.[2]

Patty Hearst was held by the group for 18 months. She made national headlines when she participated in a bank robbery on behalf of the group. At her court hearing, she claimed Stockholm syndrome and brainwashing by the group as well as threats and intimidation if she did not take part in the robbery. Some suggest she fell in love with one of her captors, but this was never proven or, for that matter, even explored since it had nothing to do with the legal proceedings. It is clear, however, in interviews with the Chibok school girls that several of these women did, in fact, fall in love with the men who kidnapped them.

In Nigeria, it is not uncommon for girls as young as 15 to marry and have children. "Wives typically require permission from their husbands to leave the house, and they have little say in family decisions or public life," according to Fatima Akilu, interviewed in an article for The New Yorker.[3]

Akilu emphasized that Boko Haram offered many of the captured girls a life of affluence, freedom and status they didn't have prior to being kidnapped. The schoolgirls that were married off to commanders with status in Boko Haram suddenly experienced a life of comparative comfort and respect.

Fatima Akilu administers a deradicalization program called the Neem Foundation. Many of the schoolgirls who were released from their captors participated in this deradicalization program upon their return to their families.

"The wives of commanders, and also women who joined the group voluntarily, were extended greater freedoms than are typical for women in the region. We usually dismiss Boko Haram as anti-women and anti-girls, but they knew that a powerful recruitment strategy was to tell women that, 'If you join our group, you can have whatever role you want,' " Akilu said. " 'Even if you want to be a combatant, we will train you to be a combatant.' "[3]

The promises made to the girls of a life of grandeur were alluring and effective. Once returned to their families, several girls ran back to Boko Haram prior to finishing the deradicalization program. These girls not only wanted to return to the riches that particular life afforded, but they knew that being back in their village, with their families, meant a life of stigma for them and their children. The children from the kidnapped girls whose fathers were Boko Haram militants would have a stigma placed on them forever. They would be seen differently by those in the community, and their mothers' who willingly married the militants would always be shunned.

"Many former wives of Boko Haram commanders were viewed with suspicion when they returned home. Their children were treated as outcasts—victims of the superstition that any child whose father was a Boko Haram member would inherit his murderous traits. Residents refused to interact with them, or to let their children play with the children of the militants."[3]

It is no wonder then that many of the Chibok girls longed for their former lives and wanted to return to their captors. Although it appeared on the international stage that this was a life of captivity and slavery for the chosen girls (those married to members), in actuality, the life offered them many more freedoms than life at home in their village. Obviously, this was not the case for every kidnapped girl. Every girl did not experience the same level of freedom and new-found power; only the girls that married men with status within Boko Haram did.

The majority of kidnapped girls were enslaved, raped, taunted and abused. For the student, it is difficult to comprehend the fact that a group of girls who grew up together, were from the same village, attended school together, and were friends and neighbors could experience such life-altering events in such a vastly different way. These girls, the chosen wives, friends who once talked and laughed on the bus on the way to school, whispered secrets to one another and volunteered to lend a hand to their neighbors, now turned away in acquiescence while their friends were tortured and abused by the same men who put food on their own table and a roof over their heads.

Some of the chosen wives almost assuredly saw their friends tortured and enslaved by their own newly acquired husbands. The authors of this text have reiterated from the beginning that a primary objective of this work is to assist the student in understanding, "not emphasizing, but understanding."

While it is no doubt difficult to comprehend these facts and understand what these girls experienced, it is necessary. These women and their thought processes involved a high degree of "survivalist mentality." In order to get through each day and cope with their new reality (a process that takes place in almost all kidnapping situations, by the way), in situations where groups are being held captive, as opposed to singular victims, a survivalist mentality akin to "me versus them" takes over and victims revert to a rationalization in which they will do anything to survive, even at the expense of their fellow captors. It is not unheard of for victims to turn on each other in this process.

Often within ISIS, terrorists assigned women within the group the task of policing other women on the street. If they found women breaking Sharia law by not wearing a veil, or moving about without a male escort or without having permission to be outside on their own, these "assigned women" would punish the female perpetrators.

Many of the world's most formidable terrorist groups, particularly ISIS, have used women in a number of ways. Women have been used as suicide bombers, a vessel in which to give birth and raise the next generation of fighters, a propaganda mouthpiece to recruit and radicalize others online, as soldiers and martyrs, and the aforementioned female police force.

Previously in this text, the authors wrote of Sajida al-Rashawi, the failed Iraqi-born suicide bomber in the Jordanian wedding celebration attack who was captured and jailed for years, by Jordanian authorities. Though Jordanian King Abdullah had intended to allow her to live out the rest of her years in prison, he finally ordered her hanged as a result of ISIS burning a captive Jordanian pilot to death. Though there is no evidence Musab Zarqawi ever actually met her face to face during the planning stages for the original attack, she became known as "Zarqawi's woman," a title he never disputed.

Within certain terrorist groups, and embedded with certain jihadis leaders, women have held and continue to hold powerful positions of influence. Bin Laden, himself, enlisted one of his wives, Siham bin Abdullah bin Husayn, to edit his writings. She was poetic and educated and often reviewed his writings for him. Bin Laden's fourth wife, Amal Ahmed al-Sadah, was a perfect fit for his life of extremism and piety. As a teenager, she often spoke about her desire to "go down in history" and made sure bin Laden knew that she wanted to become a martyr at his side. Bin Laden and Amal had a daughter, Safia. Both parents openly declared their desire for Safia to one day become active in his work and "to kill Jews."[4]

Female operatives and suicide bombers have been used by numerous terror groups all over the world. According to one Hamas leader, when asked about the role of female suicide bombers,

> **"... in the Quran, women are not only expected to share in the struggle but are even allowed to do so without the 'permission' of their 'male relatives.'"**

As for the rewards, he further opined,

> **"*Satisfaction*. In paradise, women are satisfied, which is the most important thing, because there is no competition between men and women. Everyone gets what they[4] want and are their own master. They achieve total satisfaction after death."**

Additionally, during the 1950s, the FLN (Front de Liberation Nationale) in Algeria used women as operatives in their fight against the French government. They knew that women would be effective against the French soldiers guarding checkpoints around the city of Algiers. The renowned author and counterterrorism analyst, Bruce Hoffman, discussed the FLN's choice to use women in crucial roles when fighting the French occupation of Algiers in his book, "Inside Terrorism":

> **"The campaign was spearheaded not by the group's hardened male fighters but by its attractive young female operatives .... would arouse far less suspicion than their male counterparts."**[5]

The 1966 black and white movie, "Battle of Algiers", contains a scene in which three young women carry bombs in their purses and satchels and walk to destinations/targets around the city of Algiers to carry out a terrorist attack. One woman walks through a French checkpoint with a child, knowing the soldiers would never suspect a woman or child of nefarious activity. The plan works, and the women pull off three simultaneous attacks against innocent citizens.

Such plans still work today. Routinely, around the world women within terrorist organizations are often successful in evading security or suspicion allowing them to launch attacks in the middle of crowded and guarded markets and checkpoints. The least likely suspect will generally be a winning terrorist strategy. Today, women remain the least likely suspect.

One of the authors of this book was employed at a military school for seven years as a terrorism instructor. In the early 2000s, Al Qaeda was making headlines and the United States was actively searching for bin Laden. In Afghanistan and Iraq, American soldiers were battling suicide attacks and IEDs on a daily basis. Being an effective and informed instructor required constant research on the latest terrorist tactics.

Time and time again, this research pointed to the increased and continued use of women within terrorist groups. Women were making headlines as suicide bombers in numerous attacks worldwide. Women were also being used to recruit others to the terrorist's cause.

Often women recorded videos prior to strapping on their suicide vests in which they taunted men by stating "you are 'sitting on your hands' so sisters have to step up and take your place."[6]

Women, still today, are very actively involved with terrorist groups in a variety of capacities. Women are highly influential as recruiters and wildly successful in influencing both men and women. The tactics used by these women to reach out to men and encourage them to join are quite different than that used, when they approach other women. Women appeal to men by enticing them with the adventures they will have as part of the group and the heroes they will be in the eyes of the masses.

The concept of valiant deeds and martyrdom is alluring to men. Women appeal to other women by telling them of the virtues of life within the terror group, that Allah will look favorably upon them and that they can bring honor to their family. Men and women both are often easily recruited by women, urging joining the terrorist group as their "duty" and appealing to a "higher calling."

Of interest to the student of International Terrorism is a thorough analysis of the difference in recruiting tactics, enticing women versus men. ISIS routinely posts photographs online of young jihadi fighters holding kittens and admiring beautiful sunsets in order to draw women to joining their group. Though ludicrous in concept, the marketing tactic works. Such makes the men appear kind and caring and "normal" to these young, naive women many of whom eventually join their group.

Another successful marketing strategy used by ISIS involved touting the plethora of Nutella they had within their grasp. Seemingly insignificant to the uninitiated, such is a real marketing strategy ISIS used to draw women. The tactic is a subtle attempt to emphasize "normalcy" and "humanity" as well as an inference that a life with "the group" is a life of plenty.[7,8]

When focusing their recruitment efforts on men, ISIS used images depicting guns, ammunition, stories of battle and honor and revenge, and gruesome photos of beheadings of their captors.

THE BIRTH/RISE OF NEW TERROR GROUPS

History has shown that when one terrorist group is toppled, another is generally waiting in the wings. Sometimes it is not the killing of a top terrorist leader that leads to the rise of other groups. Sometimes it is a new state policy, such as the banning of the hijab in France, or dissatisfaction with the local government by the people that stimulates a rise in followers of terrorist groups.

It is not difficult to persuade others to join these terror groups. Though the recruits are usually very young and probably not mature enough to understand the consequences, they often see themselves as unafraid to die for a cause in which they believe. In fact, they often hope to die as a martyr on behalf of the terror organization. Bin Laden told his followers of Americans, "They love life like we love death."[4]

American's often don't understand this mentality. This does not compare to an American military family being proud of their family member that died in the act of service to our nation. We understand the family celebrating these brave men and women. But for the contemporary student of this subject, it is difficult to comprehend a mother being happy that her son or daughter died in an act of martyrdom on behalf of a terror group especially when innocent civilians are the target. The mothers and fathers of these "martyrs" have a completely different and foreign (to us) perspective. In an act of martyrdom, they believe there are no "innocent" casualties, only the will of Allah, and those that perish were meant to perish for the greater good, and will be rewarded in "paradise."

NEW TERROR TACTICS

In light of the terrorist threats that we face today, it is interesting to look at past terror groups, their motives, their creed and their targets and tactics, and which of these groups were successful in bringing about the change(s) they were seeking. When examining groups such as the Sendero Luminoso in Peru, the Red Army Faction in Germany, The Grey Wolves in Turkey, the KKK and many others, one can see the evolution of terrorist tactics; how various groups chose their victims and how their weapons of choice evolve to meet their objectives.

Research indicates that terrorist methodology is morphing toward the use of low-cost, simple actions such as knives, and away from time-consuming techniques such as concocting bombs. Modern tactics seem to have adopted the philosophy of "cheap and easy," including such actions as driving into crowds of people.

In the not too distant past, terror groups often resorted to kidnappings of prominent citizens for ransom. Today, we see terrorist groups making maximum use of a 24-hour news cycle ensuring that their group and their creed are prominent on the world stage. Through the use of suicide bombers, car bombs and other exigent tactics, the world is inundated with the group and the message.

When conducting analysis of Al Qaeda from its inception through to the present day, it is easy to note shifts in tactics. Once an organized group with geographic presence throughout the Middle East and parts of Europe and far east Asia, Al Qaeda is now dispersed and grounded throughout the world.

Their preference seems to rely on cheap, easily planned individual attacks, rather than large, expensive and complicated methods of attack. Al Qaeda 3.0, a term coined by Gabriel Weimman, professor of communications from Haifa University, Israel, and visiting instructor at Wilson Center,[9] defines Al Qaeda as the "new Al Qaeda" whose methods center on using lone wolf individuals to recruit, radicalize, finance, garner sympathizers and carry out attacks on their own. Such methods have proven successful. These methods are additionally used by ISIS.

NOTES

1 McKelvey, T. (2016, April 13). Michelle Obama's hashtag quest to rescue Nigerian girls. *BBC News.* https://www.bbc.com/news/world-us-canada-35948362.
2 American Experience. (n.d.). The rise and fall of the Symbionese Liberation Army. https://www.pbs.org/wgbh/americanexperience/features/guerrilla-rise-and-fall-symbionese-liberation-army/.
3 Nwaubani, A. T. (2018, December 20). The women rescued from Boko Haram who are returning to their captors. *The New Yorker.* https://www.newyorker.com/news/dispatch/the-women-rescued-from-boko-haram-who-are-returning-to-their-captors.
4 Bergen, P. (2012). *Manhunt: The ten-year search for Bin Laden from 9/11 to Abbottabad.* New York, NY: Crown Publishers.
5 Hoffman, B. (2006). *Inside terrorism,* (p. 58). New York, NY: Columbia University Press.
6 Von Knop, K. (2007). The female jihad: Al Qaeda's women. *Studies in Conflict & Terrorism, 30*(5), 397–414.
7 Wagner, M. (2014, August 23). Apparent ISIS terrorists take photos with Nutella to seem softer, friendlier to West. *New York Daily News.* https://www.nydailynews.com/news/world/isis-fighters-photos-nutella-friendly-article-1.1914450.
8 Mosendz, P. (2015, February 19). No, ISIS doesn't use Nutella, kittens to lure female recruits. *Newsweek.* https://www.newsweek.com/no-isis-doesnt-use-nutella-kittens-lure-female-recruits-308080.
9 Weimann, G. (2014, February 27). Lone wolf terrorists. *Wilson Center.* Available from https://www.wilsoncenter.org/article/lone-wolf-terrorists.

INDEX

Made in the USA
Coppell, TX
19 January 2025

44590638R10109